DISCARD

L. W. Nixon Library
Butler County Community College
901 South Haverhill Road
El Dorado, Kansas 67042-3280

Business Math for the Numerically Challenged

D1562684

By
The Editors of Career Press

RECEIVED

AUG 26 1999

BCCC - NIXON

Business Math for the Numerically Challenged

By
The Editors of Career Press

CAREER PRESS
3 Tice Road
P.O. Box 687
Franklin Lakes, NJ 07417
1-800-CAREER-1
201-848-0310 (NJ and outside U.S.)
FAX: 201-848-1727

L. W. Nixon Library
Butler County Community College
901 South Haverhill Road
El Dorado, Kansas 67042-0230

Copyright © 1998 by Career Press

All rights reserved under the Pan-American and International Copyright Conventions. This book may not be reproduced, in whole or in part, in any form or by any means electronic or mechanical, including photocopying, recording, or by any information storage and retrieval system now known or hereafter invented, without written permission from the publisher, The Career Press.

BUSINESS MATH FOR THE NUMERICALLY CHALLENGED
ISBN 1-56414-316-3, $11.99
Cover design by Foster & Foster
Printed in the U.S.A. by Book-mart Press

To order this title by mail, please include price as noted above, $2.50 handling per order, and $1.50 for each book ordered. Send to: Career Press, Inc., 3 Tice Road, P.O. Box 687, Franklin Lakes, NJ 07417.

Or call toll-free 1-800-CAREER-1 (in NJ and Canada: 201-848-0310) to order using VISA or MasterCard, or for further information on books from Career Press.

Library of Congress Cataloging-in-Publication Data

Business math for the numerically challenged / by the editors of Career Press.
    p.   cm.
    Includes index.
    ISBN 1-56414-316-3
    1. Business mathematics.   I. Career Press Inc.
  HF5691.B897   1998
  650' .01'513--dc21

                                  97-36693
                                      CIP

650
BUS

2000 - 958

Contents

Acknowledgments

It took the effort and dedication of many individuals to put together a business math book that really explains the subject in accessible terms, but most of all, this book could not have been written without the skills and expertise of our resident math whiz, Ian Mahaney.

The editors of Career Press would like to thank Ian for the time he took to develop a math book that will be an asset for any businessperson—or anyone—who needs to brush up on math skills. For those of us who worked on the book with Ian, we can actually say that math really can be fun!

The Importance of Math in Business

Math plays an important role in many facets of our daily life. A good grasp of math will facilitate such transactions as buying a car, opening a checking account and balancing a checkbook, understanding the newspaper, or budgeting personal finances. In the business world, math is even more fundamental in that it helps you to understand sales, inventory, production schedules, payroll, and financial issues concerning your department or company. Math is so important in the business world that it's key to have a basic knowledge in order to survive. If you understand how to apply basic math functions to various aspects of your job as the need arises, you'll set yourself apart from your peers and you'll never be floundering when it comes to handling numbers. This book will help you learn the math that is essential to doing your job efficiently.

Chapters 1 through 4 address the four functions: addition, subtraction, multiplication, and division. This is the math you learned in grammar school or high school, but may have since forgotten. Each of the first four chapters covers one of the four functions, offering the basic techniques for solving each problem along with methods that will simplify the problem and save you time.

Chapter 5 deals with higher math, specifically techniques of estimation, algebra, and statistics. Learning each of these will enable you to work out further problems you encounter in your business life. Roots, exponents, fractions, decimals, and percents are also discussed, because a good grasp of these is also essential to managing the flow of numbers and documents containing them in your day-to-day business duties. Then in the last four chapters, you will learn to apply all the math you learned so far to specific business functions, such as calculating interest and interpreting financial statements, calculating payroll, and analyzing sales and inventory reports.

The purpose of *Business Math for the Numerically Challenged* is to provide you with the basic elements of math needed in business. The arithmetic and applications in each section is clearly explained and will lead you to a knowledge of math that will help you to survive in the business world and to shine among your peers. Who knows, maybe you'll become obsessively involved in understanding the true meaning of math so that you'll be influenced to buy books with titles like *Algebra of the Statistical Dimension* or *Abstract Theory of Nodal Orders*. (*I* do not know what a nodal order is, no less its theory, nor can I identify with anything abstract.)

Chapter 1

Addition

Addition is the basis of arithmetic. It is a function or operation that represents movement to the right on the number line or the process of increasing the value of numbers. When adding two numbers, say 6 + 5, the sum is the result of the first number being added to the second number—moving 5 spaces to the right of 6 on the number line; 6 + 5 = 11.

The number line displays this concept for you.

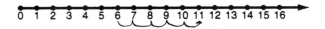

All numbers have value (6 is the value of a number in the last example shown as is 5 and 11). The base ten system grounds the value of all numbers in roots by assigning each digit a value from 0 to 9. Every digit of any number, whether the digit is a tenth (0.1), hundredth (0.01), one (1), ten (10), hundred (100) or any other digit, possesses a value from 0 to 9. The value of any number can be broken down into the value its digits possess. For example, the number 589 comprises three digits: the hundreds, tens, and ones. Each digit has a value ranging from 0 to 9, the hundreds digit holds the value 5 or five hundreds; the tens digit holds the value of 8 or eight tens; while the ones digit holds the value of nine ones. These three values in the ones, tens, and hundreds digits combine to make up the number 589. The number 1,039 consists of four digits: the thousands, hundreds, tens, and ones. The values of one thousand, zero hundreds, three tens, and nine ones combine to embody the number 1,039.

The following sample space of the number line is the area between 0 and the whole number 1 and shows that there are ten tenths of a whole number between each whole number.

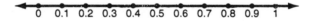

Each mark between 0 and 1 represents a tenth (mathematically considered .1 or 1/10). Notice as well that any number can be split into ten spaces. When 100 is split into ten parts, one part of that is 10, and a part of a 10 that is split ten times is considered a 1. A part of a tenth split into ten is a hundredth, the hundredths when split become thousandths. You have surely encountered the concept of splitting as division and combining as multiplication.

In grammar school and high school you learned that the base ten system is the foundation of mathematics. Every number is categorized by and comprises value and digits. The value of a number is the total it represents, and each digit—the tens, ones, tenths, hundreds, etc.—has a value within it, ranging from 0 to 9, embodying the total value of the number. Once a digit is valued at 10, the value transfers to the next highest digit. For example, in the number 10, the 10 can be considered ten ones or one ten. For the sake of simplicity and organization, we say this is one ten.

The same can be said for the number ten tens. When ten tens are combined, they become known as the simpler one hundred.

When adding two numbers together, a third number is created, and when this number is greater than or equal to 10, it is too large to fit within the parameters of a single digit (only the digits 0 through 9 can be the values of a digit), therefore part of the value of the digit is carried to the next digit. For example, when adding 9 + 8, 17 ones is the answer, but it is too large a value for the ones digit. Therefore 1 ten (or 10 ones) is carried to the tens digit and 7 ones are allotted to the ones digit. This can be summarized visually as follows:

$$
\begin{array}{lll}
 & \overset{1}{} & \\
\text{a.} \quad 9 & \text{b.} \quad 9 & \text{c.} \quad 9 \\
\underline{+\ 8} & \underline{+\ 8} & \underline{+\ 8} \\
 & 7 & 17
\end{array}
$$

In doing addition, you will often need to carry a value to a digit that also has values to be added together. The carried value is simply added to the other values and brought down to the sum of that digit and possibly carried to the next. The following example will illustrate this quite well.

When you leave for your cigarette break, you normally walk through the warehouse and head out behind the dumpster to smoke. As you walk out in the morning, an enterprising citizen calls you over and asks you to help him with his addition problem. He's lost his calculator and forgets what he learned in grammar school about addition and carrying. He estimates that he stole $556.78 worth of stereo equipment and $479.33 worth of furniture and wants to know how much he has before he heads to the pawn shop. You find it odd that he estimates the values so precisely but doesn't know how to add, but you help him with his addition problem anyway.

You explain to him that if he sets up his problem aligned vertically, he can add the two numbers together by adding each digit together and carrying any numbers needed. The first digit on the right is the hundredths (cents) and you tell him that the procedure is to add the hundredths first, bring down the sum (carrying if necessary), then proceed to the tenths, then the ones, the tens, and finally the hundreds. The hundredths involves adding $8 + 3$, which equals 11 hundredths. Since 11 hundredths is greater than or equal to 10 hundredths, we will need to split its value or carry part to the tenths digit. 1 hundredth fits nicely into the hundredths digit while 10 hundredths (or 1 tenth) is carried and superscripted above the tenths column to be added later. The tenths digits are added next. This time you will need to add three digits: $7 + 3 + 1$, which equal 11 so the ones *digit is allotted 1 (via the superscript) and 1 is brought down in the tenths digit. Adding three numbers is easy provided you think about what is occurring. It is the same as adding two numbers together twice, 7 + 3 = 10 and 10 + 1 = 11.*

Here is a demonstration of how this young entrepreneur would add his earnings.

			1		1 1
a.	$556.78	b.	$556.78	c.	$556.78
+ $479.33		+ $479.33		+ $479.33	
			1		11

d.	$556.78	e.	$556.78	f.	$556.78
+ $479.33		+ $479.33		+ $479.33	
6.11		36.11		1,036.11	

You tell him that the decimal point has no bearing on how the numbers are added, but that it is wise to leave it in place so that he won't make the mistake of claiming he has 100 times the amount of stolen goods than he actually has. There's a substantial difference between $556.78 and $55,678 worth of stereo equipment.

Keep in mind that you can and should use any short-cut possible to cut down the time necessary to complete a problem. For example, if you find that you can add two three-digit numbers together without having to add in columns, do it. If you find that estimating the results will help you find results quicker and you don't need an exact figure, by all means estimate. The point is that in math, as long as you can come up with the right answer, the steps you take to get there can vary. So use what works for you.

The final piece of advice is to use a calculator if you need quick results. If you find that you understand addition skills (or other math skills for that matter), and a calculator will quicken your results, use one. You make mistakes, I make mistakes; Newton, though he never liked to admit it, made mistakes; Einstein, too. But a calculator (if used properly) is never wrong.

Now that you have refreshed your addition skills, try the following exercises. Section A is simple addition, similar to the movement on the number line examples. Section B is a bit more advanced, involving some carrying then progressing to adding more than two numbers. Section C provides exercises similar to the addition of stolen goods and should be added carefully using the example provided.

Section A

1.   5
   + 4

2.   7
   + 2

3.   35
  + 32

4.   6
   + 2

5.   43
  + 23

6.   813
  + 2

7.   7
   + 2

8.   28
  + 11

9.   312
  + 125

10.   13
  + 6

11. 1,235
 + 234

12. 155
 + 122

13. 711
 + 240

14. 1,385
 + 4,614

15. 3,120
 + 4,719

Section B

1. 62 + 39	**2.** 39.6 + 42.0	**3.** 535 + 568
4. 136 + 45	**5.** 3,762 + 1,116	**6.** 254 + 156
7. 456 + 456	**8.** 8,526 + 1,436	**9.** 10,524 + 10,686
10. 452.1 + 451.9	**11.** 888.88 + 212.02	**12.** 1.145 + 0.955
13. 311.09 + 193.11	**14.** 486.93 + 280.22	**15.** 62.098 + 1.976

Section C

1. 347.13
    + 245.02

2. 5,564.33
    + 548.77

3. 785.813
    + 522.236

4. 456.99
    + 555.11

5. 9,325.89
    + 5,695.12

6. 99.9999
    + 11.1111

7. 1,289.94
    + 1,195.06

8. 548.34
    + 99.99

9. 483,458.1
    + 288,258.9

10. 8,549.31
    + 4,628.91

11. 528.99
    + 473.12

12. 99.099
    + 10.811

13. 418.73
    + 253.80

14. 614.33
    + 219.54

15. 8.9944
    + 13.9210

Answers

Section A

1. 9	**2.** 9	**3.** 67
4. 8	**5.** 66	**6.** 815
7. 9	**8.** 39	**9.** 437
10. 19	**11.** 1,469	**12.** 277
13. 951	**14.** 5,999	**15.** 7,839

Section B

1. 101	**2.** 81.6	**3.** 1,103
4. 181	**5.** 4,878	**6.** 410
7. 912	**8.** 9,962	**9.** 21,210
10. 904	**11.** 1,110.9	**12.** 2.1
13. 504.2	**14.** 767.15	**15.** 64.074

Section C

1. 592.15	**2.** 6,113.1	**3.** 1,308.049
4. 1,012.1	**5.** 15,021.01	**6.** 111.111
7. 2,485	**8.** 648.33	**9.** 771,717
10. 13,178.22	**11.** 1,002.11	**12.** 109.91
13. 672.53	**14.** 833.87	**15.** 22.9154

Chapter 2

Subtraction

Like addition, subtraction is incremental movement along the number line. Instead of moving to the right like addition, subtraction represents movement to the left (in the negative direction). If 3 is subtracted from 8, the difference is the location after movement to the left. $8 - 3 = 5$:

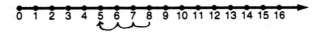

Subtraction involving numbers with more than one digit is accomplished by subtracting each bottom digit from its corresponding top digit (i.e., the bottom tenths digit from the top tenths digit). It is simple to subtract a number from another if the digits of the number to be subtracted are all smaller than the digits of the number it is subtracted from. For example:

a. 567
− 224

b. 567
− 224
343

If one of the digits of the number that is subtracted is greater than its corresponding digit on the top, a method known as "borrowing" needs to be practiced. The example of subtraction that follows illustrates this concept quite clearly.

While walking back inside after helping the thief, your boss catches you at the door and asks you if you have spare copies of the expense reports you handle. Since you have gained the reputation of caring so much about the company, your boss expects such things from you. Your boss wants to see the total shipping bill and the shipping bill of the overnight carrier. The purpose is to find out if the shipping bill of the overnight carrier is too large compared to the total of the other shipping carriers combined.

The total shipping bill is $3,456.39 and the overnight carrier cost the company $1,963.47. Since the boss wants to find the shipping bills of all the carriers combined with the exception of the overnight carrier, the job is to subtract the overnight carrier's shipping bill for the month from the total shipping bill or $3,456.39 – $1,963.47. The difference (the difference is the answer to a division problem) will give you the total of all shipping bills without the overnight carrier and will provide the same result as adding all the other carriers together. The easiest way to handle a problem such as this is to align vertically like so:

$$\$3,456.39$$
$$-\$1,963.47$$

To easier illustrate the process of borrowing in subtraction, each number is broken down into its corresponding digits (according to the base ten system):

Thousands	Hundreds	Tens	Ones	Tenths	Hundredths
3	4	5	6	3	9
− 1	9	6	3	4	7

The first step is to subtract the column farthest to the right—the hundredths column in this case: 9 hundredths minus 7 hundredths, which equals 2 hundredths. The hundredths difference can be brought down below into the hundredths difference:

Thousands	Hundreds	Tens	Ones	Tenths	Hundredths
3	4	5	6	3	9
− 1	9	6	3	4	7
					2

The tenths are then subtracted, but subtracting 4 tenths from 3 tenths results in a negative number, which is not suitable in a straightforward subtraction problems like this. (If you do not agree, you should be writing math books, not reading them.) In order to subtract the tenths, you will need to incorporate the concept of borrowing. Let's use the concept of dollars and cents to understand this. Six one dollar bills and three dimes is the same amount of money as five dollar bills and 13 dimes, it may look different, but it has the same value: $6.30. In order to derive the second from the first, you need to change a dollar bill into ten dimes—*borrow* ten dimes from a dollar. Splitting the value of a one into ten parts allows you to borrow from the ones digit for the tenths digit. To subtract the bottom tenths from the top, we need to borrow a one from the top and transfer that value to the tenths of the top, giving us 5 ones and 13 tenths on the top. In other words, we are changing the composition of the problem during the problem so that we are able to subtract every digit of the bottom from the top. The new subtraction problem looks as follows:

Thousands	Hundreds	Tens	Ones	Tenths	Hundredths
3	4	5	5	13	9
− 1	9	6	3	4	7
				9	2

If all the remaining digits of the shipping bill (top) were greater than or equal to (≥) the corresponding digits of the overnight carrier (bottom), we could finish the problem by subtracting each digit of the bottom from the top without borrowing. This is not the case, so we need to continue to borrow to make each digit adequate when subtracting the remaining digits. Rewrite the last sample of this problem so that it results in this final difference:

Thousands	Hundreds	Tens	Ones	Tenths	Hundredths
2	13	15	6	13	9
− 1	9	6	3	4	7
1	4	9	3	9	2

You can apply the knowledge of subtraction you just obtained to everyday subtraction problems. No one likes to set up a subtraction problem like we just did; it takes too much time, and subtracting within the problem is much easier once you understand the process of borrowing. Watch how superscripting the elements of borrowing quickens the pace of the problem.

a. $978.89
    − 489.92
    ‾‾‾‾‾‾‾

b. $978.89
    − 489.92
    ‾‾‾‾‾‾‾
          7

c. $9 7 $8.^189
    − 4 8 9. 92
    ‾‾‾‾‾‾‾‾‾‾
          .97

d. $9 $7$8.^189
    − 4 8 9. 92
    ‾‾‾‾‾‾‾‾‾‾
         8. 97

e. $9$7$8.^189
    − 4 8 9. 92
    ‾‾‾‾‾‾‾‾‾‾
        8 8. 97

f. $9$7$8.^189
    − 4 8 9. 92
    ‾‾‾‾‾‾‾‾‾‾
      $4 8 8. 97

Now that you have mastered the skills needed for subtraction, try your hand at the process in the following exercises. The subtraction exercises in Section A involve straightforward subtraction without borrowing. Section B involves some basic borrowing, and Section C concludes with more involved borrowing.

Section A

1.   78
       − 43

2.   569
      − 123

3.   422
       − 12

4.   989
      − 767

5.   432
       − 22

6.   333
      − 112

7.   45.58
      − 13.26

8.   81.5
      − 70.4

9.   568
      − 228

10.   79.4
      − 69.3

11.   99.281
      − 98.170

12.   589
      − 458

13.   55,789
      − 42,340

14.   90.09
      − 80.08

15.   6.199
      − 0.178

Section B

1.	33 $-\ 4$	**2.**	97 $-\ 77$	**3.**	66 $-\ 59$
4.	458 $-\ 279$	**5.**	90 $-\ 27$	**6.**	10.0 $-\ 9.9$
7.	345 $-\ 264$	**8.**	890 $-\ 781$	**9.**	412 $-\ 381$
10.	666 $-\ 577$	**11.**	1,784 $-\ 1,767$	**12.**	450.12 $-\ 394.13$
13.	80,675 $-\ 79,585$	**14.**	0.897 $-\ 0.799$	**15.**	10.892 $-\ 9.965$

Section C

1.	76.5 − 48.9	2.	456.78 − 367.87	3.	100.00 − 99.97

4.	7.77 − 6.99	5.	.789 − .598	6.	4,789.6 − 3,987.9

7.	450.21 − 399.87	8.	4,578 − 3,689	9.	5,555.5 − 4,666.6

10.	945.0 − 859.21	11.	1.254 − 1.149	12.	78.489 − 69.998

13.	88.8888 − 87.8889	14.	56.290 − 49.391	15.	1,913 − 1,906.7

Answers

Section A

1. 35	**2.** 446	**3.** 410
4. 222	**5.** 410	**6.** 221
7. 32.32	**8.** 11.1	**9.** 340
10. 10.1	**11.** 1.111	**12.** 131
13. 13,449	**14.** 10.01	**15.** 6.021

Section B

1. 29	**2.** 20	**3.** 7
4. 179	**5.** 63	**6.** 0.1
7. 81	**8.** 109	**9.** 31
10. 89	**11.** 17	**12.** 55.99
13. 1090	**14.** .098	**15.** .927

Section C

1. 27.6	**2.** 88.91	**3.** 0.03
4. 0.78	**5.** 0.191	**6.** 801.7
7. 50.34	**8.** 889	**9.** 888.9
10. 85.79	**11.** 0.105	**12.** 8.491
13. .9999	**14.** 6.899	**15.** 6.3

Chapter 3

Multiplication

Multiplication is a specific operation that is used to simplify addition problems. Multiplication is also an application of addition, but much faster. While adding 5 together five times is not such a tedious task, it can still be simplified by multiplying 5 by 5 instead. If the problem was adding 378 to itself 500 times, the task becomes quite daunting if multiplication is not used. Multiplying 378 by 500 is an application of simpler multiplication like 5 * 5 and is a lot easier than adding 378 500 times.

Here are some tips to keep in mind when multiplying:

♦ ( ) ( ) or * or • or x means multiplication. The numbers within the parentheses or around the other symbols represent the numbers to be multiplied.

♦ 3 * 4 means multiply 3 by 4.

♦ 4 * 3 means multiply 4 by 3. It differs from the above only in composition. The answer, 12, is the same, showing that you can multiply numbers in any order.

♦ 2 * 3 * 4 means multiply 2 by 3 and then multiply that product (6) by 4. The *product* is the result of multiplying two numbers together.

♦ Any number multiplied by 0 equals 0.

♦ Any number multiplied by 1 equals that number.

♦ The product is an even number if either (or both) the multiplier or the multiplicand is even; the product is an odd number only when both the multiplier and the multiplicand are odd.

The multiplication table can be used as a reference when multiplying any two numbers together that are each smaller than 10; however, it is highly advised that you have it committed to memory. Once you do, even the lengthiest multiplication problem will be easy to compute.

Table III-1
Multiplication Table

1	2	3	4	5	6	7	8	9	10
2	4	6	8	10	12	14	16	18	20
3	6	9	12	15	18	21	24	27	30
4	8	12	16	20	24	28	32	36	40
5	10	15	20	25	30	35	40	45	50
6	12	18	24	30	36	42	48	54	60
7	14	21	28	35	42	49	56	63	70
8	16	24	32	40	48	56	64	72	80
9	18	27	36	45	54	63	72	81	90
10	20	30	40	50	60	70	80	90	100

This multiplication table provides answers to multiplication of any 2 ones digits; it'll tell you what 7 * 8 equals or 5 * 9 or any two whole numbers that are less than 10. For example, to read the multiplication table in order to figure that 7 * 8 = 56, the multiplicand (the number that is being multiplied a certain number of times) is found on the left of the table (one of the numbers 1 through 10), while the multiplier (the number of times the multiplicand is being multiplied) is found at the top of the table (one of the numbers 1 through 10), and the square where both the row of the multiplicand and the column of the multiplier meet is the solution. This is demonstrated in the table below.

Table III-2
Product of 7 * 8

1	2	3	4	5	6	7	8	9	10
2	4	6	8	10	12	14	16	18	20
3	6	9	12	15	18	21	24	27	30
4	8	12	16	20	24	28	32	36	40
5	10	15	20	25	30	35	40	45	50
6	12	18	24	30	36	42	48	54	60
7	14	21	28	35	42	49	56	63	70
8	16	24	32	40	48	56	64	72	80
9	18	27	36	45	54	63	72	81	90
10	20	30	40	50	60	70	80	90	100

The product of 5 * 9 (or any other two numbers each with one digit) can also be found in the same manner by locating the multiplicand (5) in the left hand column, the value of the multiplier (9) in the top row, and the square they cross in common (45). Multiplication of complex numbers (complex numbers are numbers with 2 or more digits) is a bit more involved, but is only an extension of simpler multiplication. Whether you are multiplying 7 by 8 or 77 by 88, you are multiplying every digit of the multiplicand by every digit of the multiplier (whether you thought of it that way or not). This is a rule that applies to every multiplication problem you encounter: Every digit of the top or first number (the multiplicand) must be multiplied by every digit of the bottom or second number (the multiplier).

The following scenario will explain how complex multiplication is solely based upon the multiplication table and basic multiplication.

Your boss has at last left you to tend to your work, but as you head back to work, Billy from the warehouse stops you to seek your assistance. (It's not easy being the resident math whiz!) He's heard that you are wise in the ways of math. He's lost his calculator and recalls that you never need a calculator. He needs to find the total retail value of 9 boxes of cheap sunglasses from Taiwan. Each box has 84 pairs of sunglasses and each pair has a retail value of $3.79. You tell him that he needs to multiply three numbers together, but that he must accomplish this in two separate steps.

You tell Billy that he first needs to find the total number of sunglasses. This is done by multiplying the number of sunglasses in a box by the number of boxes. This will provide the same result as adding 84 sunglasses to itself 9 times, but much more quickly. "Complex" multiplication, you tell Billy, is the process of multiplying every digit of one number by all the digits of another.

In the example illustrated, you need to multiply 9 by every digit of the top number (84). First, multiply the ones digit of the top number (4) by 9 (the ones digit of the bottom or the multiplier). 4 * 9 = 36, but as in addition, it is too large a number to fit into the ones digit because the product, 36, consists of 3 tens and 6 ones. The ones digit is brought down just like when adding and 3 tens are superscripted above the tens digit. The final step is to multiply the tens digit on the top by the ones digit of the bottom. That's 8 * 9 = 72 tens. But what about the 3 tens that are carried to the tens digit from the ones? Billy asks if he needs to multiply that, too. You remind Billy that the superscripted 3, representing 3 tens, is already a *product,* so it needs to be added to 72 tens to result in 75 tens.

Because there are no hundreds, the 7 hundreds in 75 tens can be brought down to the hundreds column while the 5 tens are allotted to the tens digit. It is the same result as carrying the 7 hundreds to the hundreds column and multiplying the number of hundreds in the top (0) by the number of ones in the bottom (9) and then adding 7 to that: (0 * 9 = 0; 0 + 7 = 7).

Your result:

$$
\begin{array}{r}
3 \\
8\,4 \\
*\ \underline{9} \\
756
\end{array}
$$

Then you need to find the total retail value of all the sunglasses given the retail price for an individual pair and the total number of pairs. It is 756 * $3.79 (number of pairs * price per pair) or:

$$
\begin{array}{r}
\$3.79 \\
*\ \underline{756}
\end{array}
$$

The same concept applies in that you multiply every digit of the top (multiplicand) by every digit of the bottom (multiplier). The dollar sign should remain in the problem because it has a considerable effect on the outcome of the problem as the product needs to be in terms of dollars and cents. Decimal points should also be left in place lest they be forgotten, as they are a crucial component of the product.

Before you begin the problem, you remind Billy that he is to multiply every digit of the top (multiplicand) by every digit of the bottom (multiplier), but this problem differs because there are two or more digits in each the multiplicand and the multiplier. A product, in a situation such as this, is derived by creating subproducts then adding the subproducts together to obtain the product (the actual solution). A subproduct is constructed by multiplying a single digit of the multiplier (bottom) by every digit of the multiplicand (top).

Remembering to carry the proper digits, the subproducts we obtain are 2,274, 18,950, and 256,300. 18950 is the second subproduct, not 1895, because the second subproduct is the result of multiplying the tens digit of the multiplier by the multiplicand—or 379 * 50, which equals 18,950. Likewise, the third subproduct, 256,300, is the result of multiplying 7 hundreds by the multiplicand, 379. Here are the subproducts displayed below:

$$\begin{array}{r} \$3.79 \\ *\ \underline{756} \\ 22\ 74 \\ 189\ 50 \\ 2653\ 00 \end{array}$$

The final result—or final product—is the sum of all the subproducts. Remembering to carry, it is as follows:

$$\begin{array}{r} \$3.79 \\ *\ \underline{756} \\ 111 \\ 22\ 74 \\ 189\ 50 \\ +\ \underline{2653\ 00} \\ 2865.24 \end{array}$$

The decimal point is placed two digits to the left of the end digit (hundredths in this case). This is because the original problem contains a total of two numbers to the right of the decimal point in both the multiplier and multiplicand. The rule is: If there are decimal points in a multiplication problem, multiply the numbers as normal ignoring the decimals. When you have the product (the total of all the subproducts), count the number of digits that are to the right of any decimal points in the multiplier and the multiplicand. That will be the number of digits that will be to the right of the decimal point in the product. If 5.8997 is to be multiplied by 2.9, the decimal point will be placed five digits to the left of the end of the product. The product of 58997 and 29 is 1,710,913 and the product of 5.8997 and 2.9 is 17.10913.

The following problems test your newly revived multiplication skills. The problems in section A are simple, based solely on the multiplication table. Section B involves carrying and decimal points, and Section C requires the comprehension of subproducts.

Section A

1.   3
       * 3

2.   9
       * 1

3.   22
       * 4

4.   4
       * 2

5.   432
      * 2

6.   12
      * 4

7.   3
       * 2

8.   4
       * 3

9.   42
      * 2

10. 123
      * 2

11.   11
      * 8

12. 312
      * 4

13. 343
      * 2

14. 4,222
      * 2

15. 8,923
      * 3

Section B

1.	33 * 4	**2.**	2.9 * 7	**3.**	342 * 5

4.	42.8 * 7	**5.**	54.78 * 2	**6.**	34.2 * 0.4

7.	89 * 6	**8.**	125 * 7	**9.**	1,958 * 6

10.	56 * 6	**11.**	599.2 * 5	**12.**	0.97 * 0.6

13.	565 * 5	**14.**	999 * 9	**15.**	9.099 * 0.3

Section C

1.   45
   * 13

2.   74
   * 1.2

3.   33.2
   * 2.4

4.   7.8
   * 0.7

5.   456.6
   * 34

6.   289
   * 109

7.   452
   * 62

8.   1,000
   * 89

9.   46.5
   * 54.6

10.   96.34
   * 96.34

11.   5,555
   * 55

12.   789
   * 456

Answers

Section A

1. 9	**2.** 9	**3.** 88
4. 8	**5.** 864	**6.** 48
7. 6	**8.** 12	**9.** 84
10. 246	**11.** 88	**12.** 1,248
13. 686	**14.** 8,444	**15.** 26,769

Section B

1. 132	**2.** 20.3	**3.** 1,710
4. 299.6	**5.** 109.56	**6.** 13.68
7. 534	**8.** 875	**9.** 11,748
10. 336	**11.** 2,996	**12.** 0.582
13. 2,825	**14.** 8,991	**15.** 2.7297

Section C

1. 585	**2.** 88.8	**3.** 79.68
4. 5.46	**5.** 15,524.4	**6.** 31,501
7. 28,024	**8.** 89,000	**9.** 2,538.9
10. 9,281.40	**11.** 305,525	**12.** 359,784

Chapter 4

Division

In the multiplication review, you learned that multiplication is a quick way to add, but you didn't realize that you also learned the basics of division. When we complete the multiplication problem 4 * 2 = 8, we are also saying that there are two 4s in 8. Likewise, there are nine 18s in 162, and 18 * 9 = 162. Division is the inverse of multiplication and calculates the number of times one number is existent in another. To find the quotient of a division problem (the *quotient* is the answer to a division problem), you need to find the number of times the *divisor* (the number that divides) is present in the *dividend* (the number that is being divided). This can be accomplished by inverting to a multiplication problem or dividing outright. If you must divide 8 by 4, the question is, "How many 4s are there in 8?" Another way to ask this question is, "What number multiplied by 4 equals 8?" The obvious answer (even if you need to refer to Table III-1) is 2, because 2 * 4 = 8 and there are two 4s in 8. This problem can be written as:

$$8/4 = 2 \qquad 4\overline{)8} = 2 \qquad 8 \div 4 = 2 \qquad \frac{8}{4} = 2$$

It can be inverted to take the form of multiplication: 2 * 4 = 8, (2)(4) = 8, 2 • 4 = 8 or 2 x 4 = 8. Similarly, the problem of dividing 162 by 9 asks the question, "How many 9s are there in 162?" Using the multiplication properties used in the previous chapter, we know the answer to be 18 because 9 * 18 = 162. Division is simply the inverse of multiplication, and more difficult division problems are simply an extension of basic division. Dividing is much like all the other operations you've learned in that complex problems are based upon fundamental principles and solutions.

If you did not know that 18 * 9 = 162 and were to divide 162 by 9, the problem can be partitioned and simpler division will give you the answer you seek. The shape of any complex division problem is the same and looks as follows:

$$9 \overline{)\, 162}$$

Like multiplication, we will divide part of the dividend by the divisor then proceed to another part. There are 1 hundred, 6 tens, and 2 ones in the dividend, but unlike multiplication, we do not consider the 1 to be a hundred or the 6 to be a ten or the 2 a one during the course of the problem, but consider the 1 to be of greater magnitude than 6 and 6 to be of greater magnitude than 2. And again unlike multiplication, we will begin on the left side of the dividend and attempt to divide the first part of the dividend (that is, the left part of the dividend) by the divisor.

In other words, the act of dividing is accomplished by splitting the dividend and dividing the divisor into the dividend one digit at a time, beginning with the digit farthest to the left in the dividend. When dividing like this, we make it a rule that there be at least one value of the divisor contained in the part of the dividend that we are dividing. In this example, the part of the dividend has to be greater than or equal to 9 in order to divide successfully. Otherwise, we move on and divide the smallest combination of numbers on the left of the dividend that contain at least one of the dividend. 9 does not divide the first digit to the left in the dividend (1) into at least 1, so we combine it with the next digit to the right, which is 6. Now we try to divide 9 into the two digits farthest to the left in the dividend: 16. In 16, there is a whole 9 and a leftover. The leftover amount is called the remainder. Since there is one 9 in 16, we place 1 above the 6 of the dividend like so:

$$\begin{array}{r} 1 \\ 9{\overline{)\,162}} \end{array}$$

Then, to find the remainder, we multiply 1 by 9, place the result below the dividend then subtract that result from the dividend to form a new dividend that will be divided by the divisor:

$$\begin{array}{r} 1 \\ 9{\overline{)\,162}} \\ \underline{90} \\ 72 \end{array}$$

Notice how a zero is brought down next to the 9. This is because the 1 multiplied by the 9 is actually a tens digit, therefore what is being multiplied is 1 ten by 9.

The final process is to divide 72 by 9. We write:

$$
\begin{array}{r}
18 \\
9\overline{)\ 162} \\
\underline{90} \\
72
\end{array}
$$

This means that 18 is the quotient of 162 divided by 9.

Now that you understand the basics of division, we will delve into division involving decimals and a divisor of greater than 10.

Angie from Administration comes to your desk in the afternoon after you have already helped the disorderly citizen, your boss, and Billy with their math problems. Word has gotten around the office very quickly today that you are the resident genius. Angie has the assignment of analyzing the salary structure and thinks that the average salary will help her in this conquest. The average signal goes off and instantly, as it should, signifies division. She has taken the first step in adding all the salaries together, but can't find her calculator and does not remember long division. The company has 9 employees and the total of biweekly salaries is $11,956.22 so the problem you set up for her using long division is $11,956.22 divided by 9.

$$
9\overline{)\ \$11{,}956.22}
$$

To avoid any problems, you tell her that the smartest initial step is to remove any dollar signs and commas as follows:

$$9 \overline{) 11956.22}$$

The first real dividing step is to divide the first digit of the dividend by the divisor, but like the last problem and many more that you will encounter, one digit of the dividend (1) cannot be divided by the divisor. However, the first *two* digits together (11) can be divided by the divisor. There is one 9 in 11, with a remainder. So we place 1 above the second digit (1) of the dividend, multiply that 1 by 9 and place the product below the number of the dividend we divided into. Then we subtract the product from the dividend to create a new dividend, which we will then divide by the divisor:

$$
\begin{array}{r}
1 \\
9 \overline{) 11\ 956.22} \\
-\ 9 \\
\hline
2
\end{array}
$$

As in the last example, it may be easier for you to visualize the process by bringing down zeros into the product formed above. The product formed above is found by multiplying 1 (which is actually one thousand) by 9. If we instead interpreted the product as being formed by multiplying 1,000 by 9, we could arrange the product as shown below and subtract the product from the dividend to create any entirely new dividend.

```
         1
9) 11 956.22
   9 000.00
   2 956.22
```

Next, we divide the next *two* digits of the new dividend by the divisor (because the first digit of the dividend can not be divided by the divisor at least once). There are 3 9s in 29 with a remainder, so we place 3 above the 9 of the dividend and multiply and subtract like before:

```
         1 3
9) 11 956.22
   9 000.00
   2 956.22
   2 700.00
     256.22
```

Then we begin with the new dividend and divide the first digit or digits that contain at least one of the divisor, which happens when we divide the divisor into the first two digits of the new dividend (25 divided by 9). There are 2 9s in 25 with a remainder of 7, so we place 2 above the 5 of the dividend and multiply, then subtract:

```
         1 32
9) 11 956.22
   9 000.00
   2 956.22
   2 700.00
     256.22
     180.00
      76.22
```

Next we divide 9 into the next two digits of the third new dividend (76 divided by 9) and find that there are 8 9s in 76 with a remainder of 4. Then again, we multiply and subtract:

$$
\begin{array}{r}
1\ 328 \\
9)\overline{11\ 956.22} \\
9\ 000.00 \\
\hline
2\ 956.22 \\
2\ 700.00 \\
\hline
256.22 \\
180.00 \\
\hline
76.22 \\
72.00 \\
\hline
4.22
\end{array}
$$

Notice that the decimal place is back in the quotient. In the quotient, the decimal is placed directly above the decimal of the dividend. Now we disregard the decimal point and continue to divide and find that there are 4 9s in 42 with a remainder. Then we multiply and subtract:

$$
\begin{array}{r}
1\ 328.4 \\
9)\overline{11\ 956.22} \\
9\ 000.00 \\
\hline
2\ 956.22 \\
2\ 700.00 \\
\hline
256.22 \\
180.00 \\
\hline
76.22 \\
72.00 \\
\hline
4.22 \\
3.60 \\
\hline
.62
\end{array}
$$

Again, we divide and find that there are 6 9s in 62, with a remainder, then find the remainder by multiplying and subtracting:

$$
\begin{array}{r}
1\,328.46 \\
9)\,\overline{11\,956.22}\ \ 0 \\
\underline{9\,000.00} \\
2\,956.22 \\
\underline{2\,700.00} \\
256.22 \\
\underline{180.00} \\
76.22 \\
\underline{72.00} \\
4.22 \\
\underline{3.60} \\
.62 \\
\underline{.54} \\
.08\ \ 0
\end{array}
$$

Notice how a 0 is added to the original and newest dividend in the thousandths digit. This is because 9 will not divide 8 into a number greater than 1, so the next step is to divide 80 by 9. An additional 0 at the end of the dividend does not change the value or magnitude of the dividend because it is placed to the right of the decimal point and any other digit. 80 divided by 9 equals 8 with a remainder. Then multiply and subtract again.

```
          1 328.46  8
    9)11 956.22  0
       9 000.00
       2 956.22
       2 700.00
         256.22
         180.00
          76.22
          72.00
           4.22
           3.60
            .62
            .54
            .08  0
            .07  2
            .00  8
```

This process of adding zeroes to the end could go on and on—and does in this example. If there comes a time when the divisor does not divide evenly (that is, without a remainder) after two digits to the right of the decimal, we can round to the hundredths digit. If the thousandths digit is 4 or less, then we can round down, which means that the hundredths digit remains the same. If the thousandths digit is greater than or equal to 5 then we round up, which means that we increase the value of the hundredths digit by 1 hundredth. In the above example of finding the average biweekly salary, we round up because the thousands digit is valued at 8 so that the final average is $1,328.47.

In a division exercise when there is a number other than 0 to the right of the decimal point in the divisor, before dividing we need to adjust the divisor and the dividend so that the divisor is a whole number. Multiplying both the divisor and the dividend by the same number will not change the quotient and multiplying by a multiple of 10 (10, 100, 1,000) makes division much simpler. For example, in the following problem:

$$3.53 \overline{)\ 81.62}$$

we multiply both the divisor (3.53) and the dividend (81.62) by 100 to eliminate the decimal point, then divide.

3.53 * 100 = 353   81.62 * 100 = 8162

Thus the new division problem becomes:

$$353 \overline{)\ 8162}$$

Another way to look at this is that the decimal point in the divisor is moved to the right the number of times it takes to make the divisor a whole number. So without actually multiplying the dividend and divisor, simply move the decimal to the right in the divisor the number of spaces needed to make it a whole number, then move the decimal in the dividend an equal number of spaces to the right. Here is an example:

$$2.83 \overline{)\ 88.29\,4}$$

If there is a decimal in the divisor, but not in the dividend, then add zeros to the dividend. That is, if you move the decimal two spaces to the right in the divisor, add two zeros to the dividend, like so:

$$2.83 \overline{)8829400}$$

The exercises on the following pages will help you hone your division skills, starting with basic exercises in Section A, and advancing to more complex ones in Sections B and C.

Section A

1. $4 \overline{)48}$ 2. $3 \overline{)72}$ 3. $7 \overline{)35}$

4. $5 \overline{)105}$ 5. $3 \overline{)1,545}$ 6. $11 \overline{)121}$

7. $12 \overline{)672}$ 8. $5 \overline{)485}$ 9. $6 \overline{)282}$

10. $9 \overline{)288}$ 11. $10 \overline{)1,890}$ 12. $3 \overline{)186}$

Section B

1. $8 \overline{)48}$ 2. $3 \overline{)153}$ 3. $12 \overline{)144}$

4. $18 \overline{)378}$ 5. $8 \overline{)1,545}$ 6. $6 \overline{)100}$

7. $12 \overline{)96}$ 8. $11 \overline{)1012}$ 9. $13 \overline{)169}$

10. $100 \overline{)1200}$ 11. $6 \overline{)325}$ 12. $5 \overline{)8265}$

Section C

1. $8 \overline{)\ 1{,}012}$　　**2.** $20 \overline{)\ 999}$　　**3.** $100 \overline{)\ 1{,}598}$

4. $4.5 \overline{)\ 89.6}$　　**5.** $98 \overline{)\ 1{,}354}$　　**6.** $66 \overline{)\ 656}$

7. $8.3 \overline{)\ 78.9}$　　**8.** $1.0 \overline{)\ 45}$　　**9.** $9.8 \overline{)\ 200}$

10. $89 \overline{)\ 450}$　　**11.** $1.22 \overline{)\ 1{,}982.5}$　　**12.** $2.2 \overline{)\ 789.2}$

Answers

Section A

1. 12	**2.** 24	**3.** 5
4. 21	**5.** 515	**6.** 11
7. 56	**8.** 97	**9.** 47
10. 32	**11.** 189	**12.** 62

Section B

1. 6	**2.** 51	**3.** 12
4. 21	**5.** 193.13	**6.** 16.67
7. 8	**8.** 92	**9.** 13
10. 12	**11.** 20.31	**12.** 1,653

Section C

1. 126.5	**2.** 49.95	**3.** 15.98
4. 19.91	**5.** 13.82	**6.** 9.94
7. 9.506	**8.** 45	**9.** 20.41
10. 5.06	**11.** 1,625	**12.** 358.73

Fractions, decimals, percents, and ratios

You have already learned a bit about fractions, decimals, percents, and ratios while learning of division and how the divisor relates to the dividend. *Fractions, decimals, percents,* and *ratios* are all terms that describe a number as the part of a whole. A fraction describes two numbers in proportion to one another. For example,

$$\frac{68}{89}$$

In this fraction, 68 is the part and 89 is the whole.

To find the value of a fraction such as the one displayed above, divide. 68/89 = 0.7640 ≈ 0.76.

The fraction divided is the decimal value 0.76, the representative of the value of the fraction as a part of one. 68 parts of 89 (the fraction) is equal in value to .76 parts of 1.

A percent is the part of 100. To find a percent from a decimal, you need to multiply the decimal by 100, the percent of the example is .76 * 100 = 76% or 76 parts of 100.

The following guidelines summarize the methods used to transfer between these relationships:

♦ To find a decimal from a fraction—divide the fraction. The numerator is the dividend and the denominator is the divisor.

♦ To find a percent from a fraction, divide the fraction and multiply by 100.

- To find a fraction from a decimal, multiply the decimal by the original base to find the numerator—89 is the original base in the above example. The answer is the numerator in the fraction. If you do not know the base number, then it will be impossible to find the fraction form of a decimal.

- To find a percent from a decimal, multiply by 100.

- To find a fraction from a percent, divide the percent by 100 to determine the decimal then multiply the decimal by the base to find the numerator and arrange the numerator above the base. Like finding a fraction from a decimal, you need to know the base in order to pursue the fraction.

- To find a decimal from a percent, divide by 100.

A ratio is similar to a fraction in that it shows the relationship between two numbers. The ratio of 68/89 is 68:89. To show the part of one that it represents, the ratio is divided as a fraction: 68/89 = 0.76.

Arithmetic and fractions

The following are a few rules that will help you to add, subtract, multiply, and divide fractions:

Adding fractions. When adding fractions, you may add the numerators together and place the sum over the denominator if the denominators are equal. For example, if you were to add 4/9 and 2/9, you could write it like so:

$$4/9 + 2/9 = 6/9$$

When adding fractions that have different denominators, you must find a common denominator. Huh? A common denominator is a denominator that is a multiple of both of the original denominators. (That is, they each divide the common denominator by a whole number.) The simplest common denominator is found by multiplying the two denominators together. Then you need to adjust each numerator so that the numerator is increased equally in value as its respective denominator.

For example, if you were to add 2/5 and 3/4, the first step would be to find the common denominator. This is found by multiplying both denominators together, 5 * 4 = 20. The base of your answer will be 20. In order to add the numerators together you need to adjust the numerators in proportion to the increase in their respective denominators. The denominator of the first fraction, 2/5, is multiplied by 4 to obtain 20, therefore the numerator should be multiplied by 4, resulting in 8/20. The denominator of the second fraction, 3/4, was multiplied by 5 to obtain 20, therefore the numerator should also be multiplied by 5 to maintain the fraction at the same value, resulting in 15/20. Now it is possible to add the two fractions, because they have the same denominator. Thus, 2/5 + 3/4 would become:

$$8/20 + 15/20 = 22/20 = 1\ 2/20 = 1\ 1/10$$

Subtracting fractions. When subtracting fractions, subtract the numerators if the denominators are equal. For example:

$$13/16 - 4/16 = 9/16$$

If you are to subtract fractions where the denominators are different, you follow a similar process to adding fractions with different denominators. You must find a common denominator and then subtract. Here's an example that will help familiarize you with the process:

$$(5/8) - (2/9)$$

A common denominator of 8 and 9 is 72 because 8 * 9 = 72 so we need to adjust each numerator in proportion to its respective denominator:

$$(5 * 9)/(8 * 9) - (2 * 8)/(9 * 8) = 29/72$$

or

$$(45/72) - (16/72) = 29/72$$

Multiplying fractions. A relief comes when multiplying fractions. You may simply multiply the numerators together and the denominators together to create the product:

$$(3/4) * (5/6) = (3 * 5) / (4 * 6) = 15/24$$

Dividing fractions. If you are dividing fractions, you need to invert one of the fractions and multiply using the above multiplication rule. This makes sense because division is the inverse of multiplication. You may invert either fraction, but if you make it a rule to invert the second then you won't forget that step. For example, here is a division problem involving fractions:

$$(1/4) \div (1/3) = (1/4) * (3/1) = (1 * 3)/(4 * 1) = 3/4$$

For practice in applying these rules regarding fractions, percents, decimals, and ratios, complete the exercises in Sections D, E, F, and G on the following pages. The answers follow.

Section D

In the following, find the decimal and percent values from the fractions given.

1.	1/8	2.	3/8	3.	5/8
4.	6/9	5.	9/15	6.	12/18
7.	31/32	8.	40/46	9.	5.5/8
10.	120/757	11.	23/26	12.	91/219

Section E

In the following, find the fractions and percent values from the decimals given, assuming in all cases that the base is 77.

1.	0.143	2.	0.99	3.	1.30
4.	1.29	5.	12.99	6.	2.60
7.	0.73	8.	0.29	9.	3.25
10.	2.00	11.	0.13	12.	3.90

Section F

In the following, find the decimal and fraction values from the percents, assuming that the base is 20.

1.	95%	2.	97.5%	3.	75%
4.	55%	5.	10%	6.	82.5%
7.	155%	8.	200%	9.	340%
10.	5%	11.	65.05%	12.	71%

Section G

In the following add, subtract, multiply, or divide as instructed.

1. (1/5) + (3/5)
2. (2/7) + (3/7)
3. (4/7) + (3/8)
4. (4/9) + (3/10)
5. (3/4) − (1/4)
6. (5/6) − (1/6)
7. (6/7) − (8/11)
8. (7/8) − (3/5)
9. (4/5) * (3/7)
10. (1/8) * (4/13)
11. (7/17) ÷ (7/15)
12. (2/3) ÷ (4/9)

Answers

Section D

1. 0.125
   12.5%

2. 0.375
   37.5%

3. 0.625
   62.5%

4. 0.67
   66.67%

5. 0.6
   60%

6. 0.67
   66.67%

7. 0.97
   96.88%

8. 0.87
   86.96%

9. 0.69
   68.75%

10. 0.16
    15.85%

11. 0.88
    88.46%

12. 0.42
    41.55%

Section E

1. 11/77
   14.3%

2. 76/77
   99%

3. 100/77
   130%

4. 99/77
   129%

5. 1,000/77
   1,299%

6. 200/77
   260%

7. 56/77
   73%

8. 22/77
   29%

9. 250/77
   325%

10. 154/77
    200%

11. 10/77
    13%

12. 300/77
    390%

Section F

1.	19	2.	19.5	3.	15
	0.95		0.975		0.75
4.	11	5.	2	6.	16.5
	0.55		0.10		0.825
7.	31	8.	40	9.	68
	1.55		2.00		3.40
10.	1	11.	13.01	12.	14.2
	0.05		0.6505		0.71

Section G

1.	4/5	2.	5/7	3.	53/56
4.	67/90	5.	2/4	6.	4/6
7.	10/77	8.	11/40	9.	12/35
10.	4/104	11.	105/119	12.	18/12

Chapter 5

Upper Level
Math Review

The math featured in this chapter is more complex than the math covered so far, but equally important in the pursuit of business applications. The contents of this chapter, rounding and estimating numbers, averages, and algebra, are applications of arithmetic. All the math learned in this and the preceding chapters will be used in the business applications that follow.

Rounding numbers

Frequently, the accuracy of the answer to an arithmetic problem is not a major concern. Instead, speed is the main concern, and your ability to estimate and round numbers can shorten the time it takes to complete a problem. As shown in the last division problem of Section C in Chapter 4, we rounded the quotient to the hundredths digit because the thousandths digit and beyond is not considered significant when determining a pay scale. In some instances, the thousandths value may be important, such as when determining the winning time in the Olympic 100 meter dash or 50 meter freestyle events. In other circumstances, it may not be important to quantify the ones digit or even up to the thousands digit or higher. The sales figures for billion-dollar firms may be estimated to the hundred thousands digit or even the millions. If obtaining exact answers is not essential, then it may be worthwhile to estimate.

When rounding to a certain digit, you round up if the digit to the right is greater than or equal to five, and you round down when the digit to the right is less than or equal to four. Here are the basic guidelines:

◆ **Rounding to the tens** means making the tens digit the last digit with a significant number for accuracy.

$$62 \rightarrow 60$$
$$1{,}256 \rightarrow 1{,}260$$
$$784 \rightarrow 780$$
$$4 \rightarrow 0$$

◆ **Rounding to the thousands** means making the thousands digit the last digit with a significant number for accuracy:

$$192 \rightarrow 0$$
$$89{,}586 \rightarrow 90{,}000$$
$$800 \rightarrow 1{,}000$$
$$9{,}784{,}456 \rightarrow 9{,}784{,}000$$

◆ **Rounding to the hundredths** means making the hundredths digit the last digit with a significant number for accuracy.

$$1{,}890.67 \rightarrow 1{,}890.67$$
$$91.524589 \rightarrow 91.52$$
$$0.981 \rightarrow 0.98$$
$$5.0049 \rightarrow 5.00$$

Section A

Round the following to the nearest hundredth.

1.	0.4589	_____	**7.**	0.999	_____
2.	4.095	_____	**8.**	2.005	_____
3.	1.999	_____	**9.**	9.561	_____
4.	4.56	_____	**10.**	0.784	_____
5.	6.991	_____	**11.**	45.002	_____
6.	9.949	_____	**12.**	789.457	_____

Section B

Round the following to the nearest hundred.

1.	7,890	_____	**7.**	12,442	_____
2.	897,120	_____	**8.**	100	_____
3.	7,894.2	_____	**9.**	78.99	_____
4.	4,651	_____	**10.**	15.99	_____
5.	44.78	_____	**11.**	465	_____
6.	89,368.1	_____	**12.**	456.004	_____

Section C

Round the following to the nearest ones.

1. 1.01 _____   7. 0.50 _____

2. 81.2 _____   8. 0.49 _____

3. 45.0 _____   9. 78.2 _____

4. 77.5 _____   10. 69.49 _____

5. 6,894.43 _____   11. 12.35 _____

6. 0.49 _____   12. 0.454 _____

Section D

1. Add the following numbers then round to the nearest tenth.

   45.90, 6.458, 23.55

2. Round the following numbers to the nearest tenth then add.

   45.90, 6.458, 23.55

3. Subtract the first two numbers from the third number and then round to the nearest hundred.

   9,786, 4,970, 45,897

4. Round all three numbers to the nearest hundred then subtract the first two from the third.

   9,786, 4,970, 45,897

5. Multiply $12.65 by 45 then round to the nearest dollar.

6. Round $12.65 to the nearest dollar then multiply by 45.

7. Divide $67 by 3 kids then round to the nearest dollar.

8. Divide $67 by 3 then round to the nearest five-dollar bill.

Section E

1. Your firm produces three models, the X601, X-602, and X-603, all of which sell quite well—in the millions each year. Your firm estimates sales to the 100 thousands, and sales for each model this year are $5,789,075, $10,546,248, and $9,852,554, respectively. Find the estimated sales for each model this year.

2. Based upon the sales of model X-603 ($9,852,554 this year) and assuming sales will stay constant (sales will be the same next year and in two years, etc.), find the estimated sales for the next two and a half years.

3. Find the average monthly estimated sales last year for model X-602.

4. The production department of your firm has a monthly budget of $15,255. Find the annual budget rounded to the hundreds digit.

Answers

Section A

1. 0.46	**2.** 4.10	**3.** 2.00
4. 4.56	**5.** 6.99	**6.** 9.95
7. 1.00	**8.** 2.01	**9.** 9.56
10. 0.78	**11.** 45.00	**12.** 789.46

Section B

1. 7,900	**2.** 897,100	**3.** 7,900
4. 4,700	**5.** 0	**6.** 89,400
7. 12,400	**8.** 100	**9.** 100
10. 0	**11.** 500	**12.** 500

Section C

1. 1	**2.** 81	**3.** 45
4. 78	**5.** 6,894	**6.** 0
7. 1	**8.** 0	**9.** 78
10. 69	**11.** 12	**12.** 0

Section D

1. 75.9
2. 76, notice how it differs from the above.
3. 31,100
4. 31,100, notice how the answer does not differ from that above, but the methodology does.

5. $569
6. $585, notice how it differs from problem # 5.
7. $22
8. $20

Section E

1. $5,800,000, $10,500,000, and $9,900,000.

2. Either $24,800,000 or $24,600,000 depending on when you round. If you round the sales for one year then multiply by 2.5, you then round again with the product to result in $24,800,000. If you multiply the actual sales figure by 2.5 then round only once, your answer is the more accurate $24,600,000. It is recommended that you use the second method, because the estimation is always closer to the actual result.

3. $900,000 if you round before dividing by 12 and then after, or if you divide the actual sales figure by 12 then round only once. Again, it is preferable to use the second method, because the estimation is always closer to the actual result.

4. $183,100 if you round only after you multiply 12 by $15,255 (this is the correct way), or $183,600 if you were to round the monthly budget first, then multiply by 12.

Averages and statistics

Averages constitute basic statistics, and the mean is the most frequently used average. The mean is a number that is representative of the size of a set of numbers. The example in which your manager wanted to find the average cost of a phone line is an example of the mean. Means are often used in business to calculate a value that is representative of a number of samples, and it is found by adding the samples together and dividing by the number of samples.

For instance, the average salary example on page 53 illustrates this well as you and Angie found the bi-weekly salary mean. Adding the salaries together then dividing by the number of people provides the mean bi-weekly salary. Here is another example of a mean: If the sales department has four computers, the marketing department has six computers, the production department has nine, the finance department has four, and the administration department has 12, the mean of computers per department is found by adding the computers each department has, then dividing by five, the total number of departments:

$$
\begin{array}{r}
4 \\
6 \\
9 \\
4 \\
+12 \\
\hline
35
\end{array}
$$

$$35/5 = 7$$

Seven computers per department is the mean.

The mode and median are also forms of averages that are commonly used. The *mode* is the value found most frequently in a sample. In the sample used to demonstrate the mean, {4,6,9,4,12}, the mode is 4. The *median* finds the number of the sample that is exactly in the middle. The median of the above example set of numbers, {4,6,9,4,12}, is 6 because if these numbers are put into size order comparative to one another, 6 falls exactly in the middle. (In comparative size, {4,4,6,9,12}.) If there is an even quantity of numbers in the sample, then to find the median, add the two numbers that fall in the middle of the sample and divide the sum by 2. This rule applies regardless of the disparity between the numbers in the sample. For example, should the 12 have been a 25 in this sample, the median would still be 6. The median differs from the mean in that the median does not find an average based upon magnitude, but rather based upon comparative size within a set of numbers.

The mean, median, and mode are defined in the manner above, regardless of the set of numbers we are dealing with. These three statistical measures are simple, but they are also the most important because they are prevalent in further statistics and relevant in all statistical quantities.

The following sets of exercises should provide useful practice in finding basic statistics.

Section F

Find the mean of the following samples.

1. {22, 45, 478} _____   **6.** {456, 123, 321} _____

2. {8/7, 5/7, 5/7} _____   **7.** {5, 2, 8, 1, 0.5} _____

3. {789, 45.2 ,78} _____   **8.** {444, 555, 666} _____

4. {5/2, 6/9, 0.25} _____   **9.** {80, 70, 60, 2} _____

5. {500, 567, 600} _____   **10.** {0.2, 0.3, 0.45} _____

Section G

Find the mean, median, and mode of the following samples of numbers.

	mean	median	mode
1. {45, 45, 65, 78}	_____	_____	_____
2. {4.2, 46, 100, 100}	_____	_____	_____
3. {10, 12, 11, 10}	_____	_____	_____
4. {100, 1}	_____	_____	_____
5. {199, 1,000, 245}	_____	_____	_____
6. {0.23, 0.23, 0.23}	_____	_____	_____
7. {0.5, 0.67, 0.33}	_____	_____	_____
8. {25, 5, 12, 5}	_____	_____	_____
9. {2, 2, 3, 3, 5, 5}	_____	_____	_____
10. {12, 9, 3, 6}	_____	_____	_____

Answers

Section F

1.	181.67	6.	300
2.	6/7 or 0.86	7.	3.3
3.	304.07	8.	555
4.	1.14	9.	53
5.	555.67	10.	0.32

Section G

1. Mean: 58.25; median: 55; mode: 45
2. Mean: 62.55; median: 73; mode: 100
3. Mean: 10.75; median: 10; mode: 10
4. Mean: 50.5; median: 50.5; mode: none
5. Mean: 481.33; median: 245; mode: none
6. Mean: 0.23; median: 0.23; mode: 0.23
7. Mean: 0.5; median: 0.5; mode: none
8. Mean: 11.75; median: 8.5; mode: 5
9. Mean: 3.3; median: 3; mode: none
10. Mean: 7.5; median: 7.5; mode: none

Algebra

Basic algebra is an application of basic arithmetic. When the time arises that an arithmetic problem is not stated in a way that is easily solved, algebra can help you find a solution by manipulating the problem. This division exercise shows an example of how algebra can be used:

$$4.5 \overline{) 86.6}$$

In this exercise, a number with a value after the decimal is expected to be divided into the dividend. Because this would significantly complicate the problem, I explained that you can multiply both the divisor and the dividend by 100, which will eliminate the number to the right of the decimal. This is altering the problem from its original and inoperable state into a new problem that is quite obviously divisible. Algebra changes the state of this problem from one that is inoperable to one that is possible by multiplying both sides of the division problem by 100.

Often, an algebraic problem is encountered in the form of an equation. For example, an addition problem can be set up as an algebraic problem. Addition portrays the simplest of algebraic equations. If you were to add 4 + 3 + 2, you can set this up as an algebraic problem with the answer being an unknown, and you need to solve for that unknown. Say X is the unknown, so the problem looks as follows:

$$4 + 3 + 2 = X$$

If we subtract 2 from both sides of the equation, we eliminate the 2 from the left side, but also subtract it from the right side to obtain:

$$4 + 3 = X - 2$$

Then again if we subtract 3 from both sides and then 4, we obtain 0 on the left and $X - 2 - 3 - 4 = X - 9$ on the right:

$$0 = X - 9$$

If we then add 9 to both sides, the result is $X = 9$, the same as adding $2 + 3 + 4 = 9$.

The first two problems under this section labeled "algebra" were algebraic, believe it or not. They were simple, I grant you, but they exemplified two points of algebra very well: 1) Algebra involves changing the appearance of a problem so that it will favor you and be simpler to solve, and 2) algebra includes the use of an unknown, X in the case of the last problem. The next example is a bit more engaging, but remember the simple algebraic qualities that were so easy to follow before.

The VP's assistant, Sharon, shows up at your cubicle with a problem that has resulted from her snooping around the office. She has overheard the HR people discussing in their humorous ways the salary paid to Sharon's co-worker and fellow assistant, Gary. One said to another, "Sharon's yearly salary is half of Gary's salary plus $8,800." Sharon is quite flustered and doesn't know what

*to make of this. She asks you if you would help
her to find Gary's pay. She vaguely remembers
that algebra may be a part of finding the answer,
but hasn't the faintest clue how to attack the problem. You tell Sharon, "No problem, just tell me
your salary and I'll set it up for you."*

If Sharon makes $24,200, Sharon's salary as com-
pared to Gary's can be set up as follows (translated into
algebraic terms):

Sharon's Salary = $24,000 = G / 2 + $8,800

If we solve for the unknown of this equation, G,
which is Gary's salary, then we will have the answer
Sharon is seeking: the amount of Gary's salary. The first
thing we can do is subtract $8,800 from both sides of our
algebraic equation so that we eliminate part of the
problem on the side where G is. Subtracting results in
the following:

$$24,000 = G / 2 + $8,800$$

$$24,000 - $8,800 = G / 2 + $8,800 - $8,800$$

$$15,200 = G / 2$$

The next step is to eliminate 2 on the right side so
that we have an answer for G. We do this by multiplying
both sides of the equation by 2:

$$15,200 = G / 2$$

$$($15,200) * 2 = (G / 2) * 2$$

$$30,400 = G$$

So Sharon's co-worker earns $30,400 a year.

So the object, when constructing an algebraic problem, is to build as part of the problem an unknown that we will then solve. Here is a summary of algebraic properties that you can use to change the composition of a problem you cannot complete.

+ You may add, subtract, divide, or multiply both sides of the equation by the same number without changing the answer of the problem.

+ The order of adding and multiplying can be reversed. In other words, 6 * 9 equals the same product as 9 * 6 (54). This is known as the *commutative property*. Subtraction and division are not commutative.

+ The *associative property* is a continuation of the commutative property. It states that three numbers can be added or multiplied in any order. For instance, if you need to add or multiply 7, 8, and 9, it does not matter which two you add or multiply together first, 7 + 8 = 15 + 9 = 24, 8 + 9 = 17 + 7 = 24, etc.; 7 * 8 = 56 * 9 = 504, 8 * 9 = 72 * 7 = 504, etc.

+ The *distributive property* is somewhat more complicated and is better described with an example. Multiplication is distributed over addition because it can portion the value of the problem like so: 4(6 + 7) = 4(6) + 4(7) = 52. This is a useful algebraic property because you can portion a problem to make it easier. For instance, if you need to multiply 12 by 6, it may be easier to multiply 10 by 6 and 2 by 6 then add them together, $12 * 6 = 6(12) = 6(10 + 2) = 6(10) + 6(2) = 60 + 12 = 72$. It is a lot easier and quicker if you can do it in your head!

♦ You may combine like terms. For example, if you need to add the total amount of money you have in your wallet, you may group the money into sorts and then count it. Combine the quarters into a total, the one dollar bills into a total, and the 20 dollar bills into a total. If you have 3 twenties, 6 ones, and 15 quarters, you can total the money you have by adding the twenties, ones, and quarters separately. You have $60 in twenties, $6 in ones, and $3.75 in quarters, and added together the result is $69.75. An algebraic example is the combining of numerators or fractions. You can add or subtract the numerators of like bases. If you encounter the algebra problem $2/X + 3/X = 15$, you can first combine the like base into $2/X + 3/X = 5/X = 15$ and then multiply both sides by X and divide both sides by 15:

$$5 / X = 15$$

$$(5 / X) * X = 15 * X$$

$$5 = 15X$$

$$5/15 = (15X) / 15$$

$$1/3 = X$$

This basic property of algebra can be extremely useful as you can group certain terms (batches or sorts) by type.

Now that you're an algebra whiz, try your skill at solving the following problems.

Section H

The following exercises will help you with your algebra skills. Before you begin to solve the problems, you will need to translate them into algebra (the translations are supplied before the answers).

1. You are not normally involved with ordering supplies, but today the chore has fallen upon you. From a total order of $568.90, you find paper amounting to $123.67 to be deficient and therefore returnable. Find the total of the new order once the paper has been returned.

2. Your firm's top five sales reps have averaged sales of 978 air conditioners on your top model. Find the total number these five sold.

3. You heard that Sharon received a raise via the HR network. If you make $23,600 and you find out that Sharon makes twice what you make minus $20,000, how much does she now make?

4. Your diverse firm produces computer chips. If you know that the firm produces defective chips at the rate of 3 per 150 and you have a batch of 345 rejected chips from the past three months, find the total number of computer chips your firm has shipped.

5. If your firm's insurance plan pays 95 percent of all medical costs and the firm pays the rest out of good gesture, and you find that the firm has paid a total of $1,347 in medical bills over the past two months, find an estimate for the total

medical bills for all employees covered for the past year, accepting that the two month total is indicative and representative of the year's total.

6. You take a political poll in your office. The poll you took of 30 people indicated that 3/5 will vote republican. There's a total of 200 employees in your office, and you feel that the poll is indicative of people's true voting tendency. Find the total number of people in your office who will vote democratic if everyone either votes democrat or republican

Translations

1. Total order = t = $568.90 − $123.67
2. X / 5 = 978
3. Sharon's salary = S = (2 * $23,600) − $20,000
4. 345 = (3 / 150) * X
5. X = ($1,347) (100/5) (6), notice that some algebra problems seem much more complex than they actually are, it's just a matter of sifting through the masses of both useful and useless information.
6. X = 200 - number voting republican
   Number voting republican = (3/5) * 200
   So X = 200 − (3/5) * 200

Answers

1. $445.23
2. 4,890
3. $27,200
4. 17,250
5. 161,640
6. 80

Exponents

At some point in your business career, you have probably dealt with exponents. Exponents are a quick expression of multiplication and are written like so:

$$5^2 \quad 2^5 \quad 3^3 \quad 4^8 \quad 12^6 \quad 6^1 \quad 7^8$$

An exponent is solved by multiplying the base number by itself the number of times the superscripted number indicates. So $5^2 = 5 * 5 = 25$ and $2^5 = 2 * 2 * 2 * 2 * 2 = 32$. Here are some other examples:

$$3^3 = 3 * 3 * 3 = 27$$
$$4^8 = 4 * 4 * 4 * 4 * 4 * 4 * 4 * 4 = 65,536$$
$$12^6 = 12 * 12 * 12 * 12 * 12 * 12 = 2,985,984$$
$$6^1 = 6$$
$$7^8 = 7 * 7 * 7 * 7 * 7 * 7 * 7 * 7 = 5,764,801$$

On occasion, you will find it easy to simplify a problem when you need to multiply or divide exponents that have the same base. Here are brief rules that apply to arithmetic and exponents:

♦ When adding two exponents, there is no shortcut. Multiply the exponents as normal then add the two products. For example, if your problem was to add $2^3 + 3^2$, you would need to complete the exponents separately, then add them together. For example:

$$2^3 + 3^2 = 2 * 2 * 2 + 3 * 3 = 8 + 9 = 17$$

♦ Likewise, when subtracting two exponents, there is no shortcut, you need to complete the exponents, then subtract, like this:

$$4^3 - 4^2 = 4 * 4 * 4 - 4 * 4 = 64 - 16 = 48$$

♦ When multiplying exponents, there is an alternative to completing the exponents then multiplying. If the bases are different, then you need to complete the exponent and multiply those products together. When you multiply two numbers that contain exponents and each has the same base, then you can add the exponents, like so:

$$4^5 * 4^3 = 4 * 4 * 4 * 4 * 4 \ + \ 4 * 4 * 4 =$$
$$1{,}024 * 64 = 65{,}536$$

which yields the same result as:

$$4^5 * 4^3 = 4^{(5+3)} = 4^8 =$$
$$4 * 4 * 4 * 4 * 4 * 4 * 4 * 4 = 65{,}536$$

♦ When dividing exponents, a similar shortcut can be used only if the bases are the same number. We can subtract the exponents of the numbers that contain the exponents when dividing two numbers with the same bases. Watch how the following division problem can simplify:

$$5^4 \div 5^2 = (5 * 5 * 5 * 5) \div (5 * 5) =$$
$$625 \div 25 = 25$$

and

$$5^4 \div 5^2 = 5^2 = 5 * 5 = 25$$

Find the solutions to the following problems containing exponents.

Section I

1. 4^7

2. 12^4

3. 9^3

4. 6^1

5. 7^8

6. 10^5

7. 4^6

8. 13^4

9. 1^7

10. 3.5^2

11. 2.5^3

12. 201^2

Section J

1. $5^3 + 5^3$

2. $4^4 + 3^4$

3. $7^2 + 2^4$

4. $8^2 + 4^2$

5. $4^5 - 3^5$

6. $5^5 - 5^2$

7. $2^3 - 7^1$

8. $145 - 5^3$

9. $4^2 * 3^3$

10. $5^3 * 5^4$

11. $3^2 * 3^2$

12. $6^2 * 5^2$

13. $5^{27} \div 5^{25}$

14. $4^3 / 3^3$

15. $23^5 \div 23^4$

Answers

Section I

1. 16,384	**2.** 20,736	**3.** 729
4. 6	**5.** 5,764,801	**6.** 100,000
7. 4,096	**8.** 28,561	**9.** 1
10. 12.25	**11.** 15.625	**12.** 40,401

Section J

1. 250	**2.** 337	**3.** 65
4. 80	**5.** 781	**6.** 3,100
7. 1	**8.** 20	**9.** 432
10. 78,125	**11.** 81	**12.** 900
13. 25	**14.** 2.37	**15.** 23

Roots

Radicals, such as square roots, cubed roots, and fourth roots are the inverse of the exponent. $\sqrt{9}$ asks the question, "What number multiplied by itself equals 9?" The answer is 3, because 3 * 3 = 9. $\sqrt{45}$ asks the similar question, "What number multiplied by itself equals 45?" and the answer is complicated to find by hand, but the answer, 6.71, is easily found with a calculator. Seeing that there is no method that can be used for finding square roots, using a calculator is the logical approach.

Third (also known as cubed roots), fourth, and other roots ask other questions. The third root of 8 is written $\sqrt[3]{8}$, and asks the question, "What number multiplied by itself twice equals 8?" The answer is 2 because 2 * 2 * 2 = 8, and thus $\sqrt[3]{8}$ = 2. Likewise, the fourth root, such as $\sqrt[4]{625}$ asks the question, "What number multiplied by itself three times equals 625?" The answer is 5. You will rarely encounter fourth roots and beyond, but now you realize how to find the solution if you encounter them.

Section K

Find the solutions to the following problems containing radicals:

1. $\sqrt{4}$	**2.** $\sqrt{16}$	**3.** $\sqrt{256}$
4. $\sqrt{55}$	**5.** $\sqrt[3]{64}$	**6.** $\sqrt[3]{6561}$
7. $\sqrt[4]{16}$	**8.** $\sqrt{80}$	**9.** $\sqrt{400}$
10. $\sqrt[3]{125}$	**11.** $\sqrt{36}$	**12.** $\sqrt{8}$

Answers

1. 2	**2.** 4	**3.** 16
4. 7.42	**5.** 4	**6.** 18.72
7. 2	**8.** 8.94	**9.** 20
10. 5	**11.** 6	**12.** 2.83

Chapter 6

Applications of Addition and Subtraction

This chapter covers basic business applications of addition and subtraction. The basics of product sales and inventory are discussed. There are many other applications to which addition and subtraction apply—many are found in the next chapter.

Product sales

Product sales is the first application we will discuss, because it can be applied to almost every type of business. Most businesses offer the buyer options on the payment terms. When you buy a CD in a record store, there are payment choices—cash or credit. The same applies to businesses or individuals buying from your business. Sometimes customers can also pay by check, and some businesses have the option of paying with a purchase order, meaning that the business, based upon its reputable past, agrees to pay in full within a certain time frame. The following table is an application of addition and asks you to total the cash paid and credit granted for each product number.

Table VI-1
Product sales

Model #	Cash	Credit	Total
X-101	$3,786.95	$9,086.12	
X-102	$2,876.87	$7,864.56	
X-103	$8,564.09	$9,798.87	

The total sales figure for each product is calculated by adding the cash sales and the credit granted together, and the totals are as follows:

Table VI-2
Product sales

Model #	Cash	Credit	Total
X-101	$3,786.95	$9,086.12	$12,873.07
X-102	$2,876.87	$7,864.56	$10,741.43
X-103	$8,564.09	$9,798.87	$18,362.96

The preceding application of addition can be administered to any pay structure. If your firm does not extend credit, credit can be eliminated and replaced with charge, COD, or check if acceptable.

Inventory

A function of addition and subtraction is to update inventory reports. The inventory of the model numbers analyzed in the payment structure in Tables VI-1 and VI-2 will be updated in the inventory report shown in Table VI-3. Inventory is updated based on sales and deliveries. A delivery increases the inventory while a sale decreases the inventory. To update the inventory in

Table VI-3, subtract outgoing shipments or sales and add the delivered goods.

Table VI-3
Inventory report

Model #	Stock 12/1	Deliveries	Sales	Stock 1/1
X-101	15,674	10,000	12,765	
X-102	34,373	0	7,876	
X-103	23,964	3,000	6,880	

The inventory report is updated for each model number by adding the delivered stock and subtracting the sold stock. For example, as shown in Table VI-4, model # X-101's stock on January 1st is found by adding deliveries during December to the December 1st stock and subtracting stock sold during December: $15,674 + 10,000 - 12,765 = 12,909$. The other stock figures follow.

Table VI-4
Inventory report

Model #	Stock 12/1	Deliveries	Sales	Stock 1/1
X-101	15,674	10,000	12,765	12,909
X-102	34,373	0	7,876	26,497
X-103	23,964	3,000	6,880	20,084

Like the sales example, the inventory report example can be used in any inventory situation as needed, and any other factors can be incorporated, such as damaged, remaindered, or discontinued goods.

Based on the information covered in this section, complete the exercises in Section A.

Section A

Answer the following questions based on the information provided in the charts.

1. Find the total sales based upon the three means of payment your company accepts.

Product sales

Model #	Cash	Credit	COD	Total
Y-208	$2,100.56	$34,000	$4,288.25	
Y-209	$456.29	$20,000	$4,278.50	
Y-301	$1,586.90	$19,800	$3,489.20	

2. Find the cash sales in the following table based upon the total sales, credit sales, and COD sales.

Product sales

Model #	Cash	Credit	COD	Total
502		$5,500	$2,485	$11,115
503		$10,000	$7,458	$24,467
504		$9,000	$0	$17,460

3. Update the following inventory report.

Inventory report

Model #	Stock 12/1	Deliveries	Sales	Stock 1/1
Y-208	21,845	6,000	5,584	
Y-209	14,125	8,000	7,121	
Y-301	38,254	2,000	12,032	

Answers

1.

Product sales

Model #	Cash	Credit	COD	Total
Y-208	$2,100.56	$34,000	$4,288.25	$40,388.81
Y-209	$456.29	$20,000	$4,278.50	$24,734.79
Y-301	$1,586.90	$19,800	$3,489.20	$24.876.10

2.

Product sales

Model #	Cash	Credit	COD	Total
502	$3,130	$5,500	$2,485	$11,115
503	$7,009	$10,000	$7,458	$24,467
504	$8,460	$9,000	$0	$17,460

3.

Inventory report

Model #	Stock 12/1	Deliveries	Sales	Stock 1/1
Y-208	21,845	6,000	5,584	22,261
Y-209	14,125	8,000	7,121	15,004
Y-301	38,254	2,000	12,032	28,222

Chapter 7

Applications of Multiplication and Division

Many applications of business are based upon multiplication and division, usually taking the basic knowledge of addition and subtraction. If you work on a timecard, you need to understand multiplication and division to understand how much you will be paid. Similarly, if you work on commission, you need to know how to apply multiplication and division to calculate correct payroll to make sure your company doesn't shortchange you.

Payroll

Payroll begins with the timecard and uses basic mathematical processes. Calculating payroll involves the basics of the four math functions.

An hourly wage is often the system used to determine what figure to pay employees. This wage per hour needs to be multiplied by the number of hours worked in a given week. Table VII-1 provides the hours worked (in military time) by an employee during the first week of January. We can find the total hours worked that week by adding the total hours worked each day. This will determine gross pay.

Table VII-1
Timecard

Date	Time in	Time out	Time in	Time out	Hours
1/5	09:03	12:07	12:42	17:02	
1/6	08:56	12:36	13:09	17:06	
1/7	09:10	11:50	12:18	16:58	
1/8	09:00	12:00	12:32	16:58	
1/9	08:58	12:20	12:57	17:02	

The hours worked each day are found by determining the total number of hours the employee was at work. It is found by adding two totals: the first time the employee clocked out minus the first time he or she clocked in, and the second time he or she clocked out minus the second time he or she clocked in during the day. For January 5th, the employee's hours are (12:07 − 9:03) + (17:02 − 12:42) = 3:04 + 4:20 = 7:24. The total hours for the remaining days and the total hours for the week are shown in Table VII-2.

Table VII-2
Timecard

Date	Time in	Time out	Time in	Time out	Hours
1/5	09:03	12:07	12:42	17:02	7:24
1/6	08:56	12:36	13:09	17:06	7:37
1/7	09:10	11:50	12:18	16:58	7:20
1/8	09:00	12:00	12:32	16:58	7:26
1/9	08:58	12:20	12:57	17:02	7:27

Total hours   37:14

In order to find this employee's weekly pay, multiply the total hours by the hourly rate, say $8.25/hour. First, the number of minutes has to be turned into a decimal. To do this, make a fraction out of the minutes (14, in this case). The fraction would of course be 14/60 because the whole is an hour, or 60 minutes. Then convert that fraction into a decimal. Here's how this is done:

$$14/60 = 60 \overline{)\ 14} = .23$$

Refer back to Chapter 4 if you need more information on this process.

In Table VII-3, we will calculate the hours and wages for the other employees to determine the company's weekly payroll expense for a particular department. In this table, total hours for each employee are rounded to the nearest quarter-hour. Some companies do not round at all while others round to the nearest quarter-hour every day.

Table VII-3
Total hours for Department A

Employee's name	Total hours	Pay rate per hour	Gross Pay
Anna	37:15	$8.25	$307.31
Jimmy	39:45	$10.25	$407.44
Sharon	36:00	$7.50	$270
William	38:30	$9.75	$375.38

Total gross pay: $1,360.13

In the event that employees work more than 40 hours a week, they must be paid for overtime. Overtime pay is one-and-a-half times the normal hourly rate. To find the overtime rate, multiply the hourly rate by 1.5. In Anna's case, her overtime wage would be $12.38/hr. If she were to work 43 hours in a week, she would be paid $8.25/hr for the first 40 hours and $12.38 for the final 3 hours, calculated as follows: ($8.25 * 40) + ($12.38 * 3) = $330 + $37.14 = $367.14.

The tax rate for payroll is also an application of multiplication and division. If a flat percentage tax is applied to all incomes, simply multiply the decimal form of that percentage by the wages earned to find the taxes that will be deducted. If the tax is determined by how much money is made (the income bracket), you need to search a little to find this information, though all companies have it. Multiply the decimal version of the percentage rate by the wages to determine the tax. Of course, you know that there may be more than one tax to deduct—federal, state, and local—but for our purposes, we'll deduct just one tax, we'll say federal. If Anna's tax bracket indicates that she will pay 26 percent of her earnings in federal taxes, her net income after federal taxes will be 100% − 26% = 74% or .74 * $307.31 = $227.41.

Tax can be determined for each pay cycle by multiplying the tax rate by the gross pay. For instance, if I am on salary and make $36,000 a year and I am paid biweekly, I am paid $36,000/26, which equals $1,384.62 in gross salary every pay period. If the federal tax bracket I am in requires 22 percent in taxes removed, I will not get a check for the gross amount, but for (1 − 0.22) * $1,384.62 = (0.78) * $1,384.62 = $1,080.00.

Payroll of salaried employees is also an application of arithmetic. Salaried employees usually receive a gross salary for the year, but there are occasions when a company will salary employees based upon the week or month.

To determine a salaried employee's biweekly pay, divide his or her annual salary (say $35,000) by the number of pay periods. Divide the base salary ($35,000) by 26, the number of biweekly pay periods in a year (52 weeks ÷ 2 = 26 pay periods). The employee's gross pay will be $35,000/26 = $1,346.15 each pay period.

To determine an annual salary based on weekly gross pay (say $400), multiply the weekly pay by the number of pay periods—52 if paid weekly: $400 * 52 = $20,800 a year before taxes are deducted.

The following example will demonstrate other topics in taxes.

You earn an income of $37,000 a year (don't rub it in). Find your take-home pay, given the following conditions:

◆ You are paid biweekly.

◆ Your federal tax bracket requires that you pay 23 percent in taxes.

◆ Your state tax bracket requires that you pay 7 percent in taxes.

◆ You have no local tax.

◆ You have $45.69 in insurance premiums and social security deducted every pay period.

◆ You invest $100 each pay period in a 401(k).

Let's take this a step at a time:

♦ Your gross biweekly pay is your salary divided by 26 or \$37,000/26 = \$1,423.08.

♦ You pay 23 percent in federal taxes or (0.23) * \$1,423.08 = \$327.31.

♦ You pay 7 percent in state taxes or (0.07) * \$1,423.08 = \$99.62.

♦ You have no local tax so none needs to be deducted.

♦ You have standard deductions every pay period from social security, insurance, and investment of \$45.69 + \$100 = \$145.69.

♦ Your take home pay is your gross pay minus all the deductions above, or \$1,423.08 − \$327.31 − \$99.62 − 145.69 = \$850.46.

Based on this explanation, complete the following exercises.

Section A

1. Find your co-worker's take-home pay for each biweekly pay period if he's paid $22,000 a year, has 19 percent removed in federal taxes, 5 percent in state taxes, 2 percent deducted for FICA tax, and $34 deducted in social security and insurance.

2. Find my take-home salary for each weekly pay period if I earn $63,000 a year, am in the 31 percent federal tax bracket, the 12 percent state tax bracket, have 5 percent removed for city taxes, and $78 removed for social security and insurance each week.

3. What is your boss's annual take-home pay if she is paid $4,500 every two weeks in gross pay and has a total of 38 percent removed in taxes and invests $200 every week.

Answers

1. $592.15 every two weeks.

2. $552.00 each week.

3. $117,000 annual gross pay. She pays $44,460 in taxes ($117,000 * 0.38), and invests $10,400 ($200 * 52). Her annual take-home pay is $62,140 ($117,000 − $44,460 − $10,400).

Commission

Commission is also a hot payroll topic. Many people, especially salespeople, have incomes that are contingent on their sales performance, i.e., how much money they make for their firm. Their income (or commission) is a percentage of the sales they generate.

If you just got a new account sales position in which you are paid $15,000 annual base salary plus 15 percent of all sales that you make, let's find the base amount you make each paycheck if you are paid every two weeks. Since you are paid every two weeks, you are paid 26 times a year and your base salary per paycheck is $15,000/26 = $576.92. For a single pay period, let's find your gross pay if you sell $8,000 worth of goods. For the pay period, you are paid 15 percent of your sales plus your base salary. You are paid 15 percent of $8,000, which is (0.15) * $8,000 = $1,200 and adding that to your base salary totals $1,200 + $576.92 = $1,776.92.

If an assistant on my sales force earns a base salary of $9,000 biannually plus 8 percent of her sales, and she sold $6,100 worth of goods for the last two-week pay period, her gross pay for that pay period would be calculated as follows: She is paid $9,000 biannually and is paid biweekly, so she is paid 13 times biannually. Her base salary is $9,000/13 = $692.31 every two weeks. On top of that she earns 8 percent commission on her sales, which came to $6,100 in the past two weeks. So in addition to her base pay this pay period, she earns commission in the amount of (0.08) * $6,100, which equals $488. Her total gross salary for the pay period is $692.31 (base pay) + $488 (commission) = $1,180.31.

Section B

Calculate the biweekly gross salaries in the following scenarios.

1. On top of your base annual salary of $19,000 you are paid 20 percent commission for all sales you make above $10,000 each two-week pay period. What is your gross pay for the pay period in which you made $20,000 worth of sales?

2. The manager of my sales division makes a base salary of $56,000 a year and earns 1.5 percent commission on all sales within the department. Find his biweekly gross income for the pay period that reflects $110,000 in sales.

Answers

1. Base salary + 20 percent commission on sales above $10,000 = $19,000/ 26 + ($20,000 - $10,000) * (0.20) = $730.77 + $2,000 = $2,730.77.

2. Base salary + 1.5 percent commission on all departmental sales = $56,000/26 + ($110,000) * (0.015) = $2,153.85 + $1,650 = $3,803.85.

Sales

Another application of multiplication and division is in determining the dollar value of product sales. To find the total amount of sales of a certain product, we will multiply the number of units by the unit price to determine total sales for a certain item. This is a set formula that can be applied to any product. If a markup or bulk pricing is involved in the sales of a particular unit, calculations will have to be done separately for each pricing category. In Table VII-4, we are finding total sales values based upon a constant price for each unit. The total sales for model # X-101 is the number of units sold multiplied by the unit price: 12,765 * $1.09 = $13,913.85.

Table VII-4
Product sales

Model #	Amount sold	Unit price	Total sales
X-101	12,765	$1.09	$13,913.85
X-102	7,876	$1.38	$10,868.88
X-103	6,880	$1.85	$12,728

You may also find it useful to find the profit of certain products. You can find your cost in a similar manner to finding the product sales. That is, by multiplying the cost of one unit by the total sold, you will find the total cost of the units sold. Then you can find profit by subtracting cost from sales. This is demonstrated in Table VII-5.

Table VII-5
Profits

Mdl #	Unit cost	# sold	Total cost	Unit price	Total sales	Profit
X	$.45	995	$447.75	$1.39	$1,383.05	$935.30
Y	$.49	988	$484.12	$1.59	$1,570.92	$1,086.8
Z	$.59	845	$498.55	$1.99	$1,681.55	$1,183

For model X, the total cost is found by multiplying the unit cost of $.45 by the number sold, 995 ($.45 * 995 = $447.75). The total sales are found by multiplying the unit price by the number sold ($1.39 * 995 = $1,383.05). Profit is found from their difference ($1,383.05 – $447.75).

Markup and markdown

Profit and sales leads to the discussion of markup and markdown. These terms refer to discounting (putting an item on sale) or deflating the price. If a product is marked down 20 percent, that means that whoever is buying it is saving 20 percent over the normal price. If the normal price is the price at which it is sold at a retail store, then the markdown is 20 percent off the retail price. Wholesalers mark up the price of an item they distribute. They buy from the manufacturer and sell to retail stores at a price above what they paid. If they mark up the price 20 percent, that means that they are making a 20-percent gross profit on the item. (It is not their total profit because they will have costs associated with their business.)

When an item is marked down, net price is the sale price and equals: retail price – (markdown decimal * retail price), or: retail price * (1 – markdown decimal). In Table VII-6, we find the marked-down price by using the latter formula. For example, the sale price for model C-47 with a 20-percent markdown is found by multiplying the retail price by 1, minus the markdown decimal. The markdown percent is 20, therefore the markdown decimal is 0.20 and the sale price for C-47 is: $695.00 * (1 – 0.20) = $695.00 * 0.80 = $556. The marked-down sale price for the other models are noted as follows:

Table VII-6
Markdown

Model	Retail price	Markdown	Sale price
C-47	$695.00	20%	$556
C-49	$36.87	5%	$35.03
C-51	$475.19	33 1/3%	$316.79

When an item is marked up, net price is the retail price and equals: wholesale price + (markup decimal * wholesale price), or: wholesale price * (1 + markup decimal). The net price in the following example is found by using the latter method. For example, the net price for model F-12 is found by multiplying one plus the markup decimal by the wholesale price, (1 + 0.25) * $118.39 = (1.25) * $118.39 = $147.99. The others are displayed as follows:

Table VII-7
Markup

Model	Wholesale price	Markup	Net price
F-12	$118.39	25%	$147.99
F-32	$110.12	66 2/3%	$183.54
F-34	$8,027.95	42%	$11,399.69

Based on what you have learned in this chapter, complete the exercises in Section C on pages 121 and 122. The answers follow.

Section C

1. Organize the following time sheet information into a table, create formulas that can sum up the weekly hours, and compute gross pay and net pay after all taxes are removed, based upon a flat tax rate of 22 percent.

Name	Pay	Mon	Tues	Wed	Thurs	Fri
Adams	$8.95	8	6	7	8	8
Jones	$9.25	6	5	7	6	7
Parker	$9.75	8	8	8	8	8

2. Find the weekly and biweekly gross and net pay from the following information.

Name	Salary	Federal %	Paid
Twain	$43,000	22%	Weekly
Moore	$23,000	23%	Weekly
Campbell	$50,900	30%	Biweekly

3. Find the net pay for one pay period for the following commissioned sales reps, based upon a flat tax of 19 percent.

Name	Base	Paid	Sales	% Comm
Smith	$12,000	Weekly	$5,000	15%
Barney	$18,000	Biweekly	$8,000	12%
Wesson	$39,000	Biweekly	$17,000	12.5%

4. Find the total sales given the following chart.

Model #	Amount sold	Unit price	Total sales
X-105	2,508	$1.99	
X-106	4,112	$2.08	
X-107	525	$3.02	

5. Find the appropriate retail price, whether a markup or markdown.

Name	Retail or wholesale price	Markup	Markdown	Sale or retail price
X-104	$8.99	12%		
X-105	$10.92		30%	
X-106	$33.25	18%		

Answers

1.

Name	Pay rate	Total hours	Gross pay	Net pay
Adams	$8.95	37	$331.15	$258.30
Jones	$9.25	31	$286.75	$223.67
Parker	$9.75	40	$390	$304.20

2.

Name	Gross pay	Net pay
Twain	$826.92	$645.00
Moore	$442.31	$340.58
Campbell	$1,957.69	$1,370.38

3.

Name	Base	Comm	Gross pay	Net pay
Smith	$12,000	15%	$980.77	$794.42
Barney	$18,000	12%	$1,652.31	$1,338.37
Wesson	$39,000	12.5%	$3,625.00	$2,936.25

4.

Model #	Amount sold	Unit price	Total sales
X-105	2,508	$1.99	$4,990.92
X-106	4,112	$2.08	$8,552.96
X-107	525	$3.02	$1,585.50

5.

Name	Retail or wholesale price	Markup	Markdown	Sale or retail price
X-104	$8.99	12%		$10.07
X-105	$10.92		30%	$7.64
X-106	$33.25	18%		$39.24

Chapter 8

Financial Statements

Financial statements are an extremely important application of business math, far too complex to be thoroughly covered here, so this chapter will simply outline the basics. If you feel that you need more information on the subject, the sister book in this series, *Business Finance for the Numerically Challenged,* will be of much help to you.

Common financial reports

There are a variety of financial statements that may be used in analyzing a firm's position or performance. The most common statements are the balance sheet, the income statement, and the cash flow statement.

Balance sheet

The balance sheet shows and explains all of the items owned or controlled by a firm, the debts owed by the firm, and public ownership of the firm. The balance sheet balances, because assets (possessions of the firm) equal liabilities (expenses and debts of the firm) plus stockholders' equity (investment by the owners).

Table VIII-1
Balance Sheet for 1997

Current Assets

Cash	$194,900	
Accounts Receivables	$243,600	
Inventory	$730,800	
Total Current Assets	$1,169,300	$1,169,300

Fixed Assets

Plant, prop, equip	$1,339,750	
Less Depreciation	$803,850	
Net fixed assets	$535,900	$535,900

Total Assets	$1,705,200

Current Liabilities

Accounts Payable	$146,200
Notes Payable	$194,900
Other Current Liabilities	$97,400
Total Current Liabilities	$438,500
Long-Term Liabilities	$194,900
Total Liabilities	$633,400
Stockholders' Equity	$1,071,800
Total Liabilities & Stockholder's Equity	$1,705,200

Income statement

The income statement summarizes the firm's operations from its economic activities and tallies the firm's profit. The benefits of the income statement include a practical look at how a firm spends its money and how profitable a firm is.

Table VIII-2
Income Statement for the Year
Ended December 31, 1997

Sales		$2,436,000
Cost of Goods Sold:		
Materials	$925,500	
Labor	$584,600	
Heat, Light, & Power	$87,700	
Indirect Labor	$146,200	
Depreciation	$53,600	
	$1,797,600	$1,797,600
Gross Margin		$638,400
Operating Expenses:		
Selling Expenses	$243,600	
Administrative Expenses	$280,600	
Total Selling &		
Administration Expenses	$524,200	$524,200
Income Before Interest & Taxes		$114,200
Interest Expense		$11,700
Net Income Before Taxes		$102,500
Income Taxes		$40,000
Net Income		$62,500

Cash flow statement

The cash flow statement shows the cash activity of the firm, the cash that moved in or out of the firm, as well as the firm's net cash inflow or outflow during the reporting period. The cash flow statement shows analysts if the firm can meet its obligations.

Table VIII-3
Statement of Cash Flow for the Year Ended December 31, 1997

Cash Flow from Operating Activities:		
Net Income (from Table VIII-2)		$62,500
Add (or deduct) items not affecting cash:		
Depreciation Expense	$53,600	
Decrease in Accounts Receivable	$10,500	
Increase in Accounts Payable	$15,400	
Net Items not Affecting Cash	$79,500	$79,500
Net Cash Flow from Operating Activities		$142,000
(after items not affecting cash)		
Cash Flow from Investing Activities		
Sale of Land	$5,000	
Purchase of Equipment	$(170,000)	
Net Cash used by Investing Activities	$(165,000)	$(165,000)
Net Cash Flow from Operating Activities		$(23,000)
(after items not affecting cash and investing activities)		
Cash Flow from Financing Activities		
Payment of Cash Dividends	(50,000)	
Issuance of Bonds	$100,000	
Net Cash Proceeds from Financing Activities	$50,000	$50,000
Net Increase (or decrease) in Cash		$27,000
Beginning Cash Balance		$167,900
Net Increase (or decrease) in cash		$27,000
Ending Cash Balance		$194,900

Ratios

Analysis of the financial condition of a firm is often based upon the relationship of certain figures of financial statements. These relationships are known as ratios and are a highly significant application of business math. They are used to make the necessary conclusions about what is right and what is wrong with a firm.

This chapter analyzes one ratio from each of the four main groups of ratios: liquidity ratios, activity ratios, profitability ratios, and leverage ratios.

A liquidity ratio indicates the ease at which a firm can convert its assets into cash. An example of a liquidity ratio is the current ratio—current assets to current liabilities. The current ratio gives an indication of a firm's ability to pay its debts when they come due.

An activity ratio shows how effectively a firm is managing its assets, for instance how long it takes to collect the credit it grants. An example of an activity ratio is the inventory turnover ratio—the ratio of sales to average inventory.

A profitability ratio indicates at what rate a firm is generating profit compared to other entities, such as sales or assets. An example of a profitability ratio is the net profit margin—the ratio of net profit to sales.

A leverage ratio compares a firm's debt to its holdings. An example of a leverage ratio is the ratio of total debt to total assets.

If we have access to a firm's balance sheet and income statement, then we can calculate the above financial ratios using the division learned in Chapter 4. For the firm XYZ, we will find all the ratios that have been discussed in Table VIII-2, based upon the information in Table VIII-1 as follows:

Table VIII-4

Firm XYZ	Account value
Sales	$2,436,000
Net Income	$62,500
Current Assets	$1,169,300
Total Assets	$1,705,200
Inventory	$730,800
Current Liabilities	$438,500
Total Liabilities	$633,400

The ratios are:

Table VIII-5

Ratio	Equation	Value	Industry Avg.
Current	Current Assets / Current Liabilities	2.67	2.4
Inventory Turnover	Sales / Avg. Inventory	3.33 X	9.8 X
Net Profit Margin	Net Profit / Sales	.0257 = 2.57%	3.3%
Debt to Assets	Total Debt / Total Assets	0.371 = 37.1%	63.5%

These ratios, along with any other additional information that is needed, such as other financial ratios deemed important, can be used to analyze the firm's performance. Here is a possible examination of the four ratios calculated:

Current ratio (current assets/current liabilities): The current ratio is high, and it's difficult to determine whether this is good or bad. As indicated earlier, this figure gives some indication of the company's ability to pay current debt. Upon initial inspection, the current ratio being somewhat high may appear good, but sometimes debt may be beneficial for a firm, that is, if the firm uses the debt to its benefit and furthers operations.

The inventory turnover ratio (sales/avg. inventory): 3.3 times is awfully low compared to the industry average of 9.8 times. The low inventory turnover should be a major concern because the firm is not getting its goods out the door, which means sales may be lagging.

Net profit margin ratio (net profit/sales): This figure is below the industry average. This is always a weakness, because below-average profits mean that the firm is not being as competitive as it should be.

Total debt to total assets ratio (total debt/total assets): Total debt to total assets is only 37.1 percent for company XYZ, as opposed to 63.5 percent for the industry. Is this good or bad? Is debt good or bad? Having debt is good if debt is used as an advantage. If the firm uses debt to increase production, then it is an advantage because the firm earns back more than it needs to pay in interest. Debt is bad if expenses are incurred that ultimately lower profits.

Financial statements can be a tricky mathematical application because they have the ability to be extremely complicated. Do not fear them, though. Use them to your advantage. If you think a certain relationship between two numbers in a financial statement (or statements) are important, calculate a ratio and use it to create your own opinion and financial summary.

Chapter 9

Investments
and Interest

When you borrow money from a lender, you must pay interest on the money that is borrowed. Interest is a percentage of money borrowed that must be paid back in excess of the borrowed amount. When you pay the money back, you pay the principle (the money that was borrowed), usually in increments, along with interest based upon a percentage over the time period in which you borrow the money.

Simple interest

Simple interest paid is found by multiplying the principle by the interest rate, and multiplying that by the time that is taken to pay back the money (number of pay periods there are), or $S I = Prt$, where $S I$ is simple interest, P is principle, r is interest rate, and t is time. The time that is taken to repay is determined by the increments that the loan is based upon—the number of months or years it will take to repay the loan. If the interest rate is 15 percent annually for 5 years then time = 5 and rate = 15 percent (or 0.15 in decimal form). This can also be broken down into rates per month, in which case the 15 percent annual interest rate would be divided by 12 to get the monthly rate: 15% / 12 = 1.25%.

The number of monthly payment cycles would be 5 years * 12 (months per year) = 60 months.

So the interest paid on a principle of $20,000 would be calculated as follows:

annually: $\quad$ S I = $20,000 * (0.15) * 5 = $15,000

monthly: $\quad$ S I = $20,000 * (0.0125) * 60 = $15,000

The total to be repaid is the principle + interest:

$$\$20{,}000 + \$15{,}000 = \$35{,}000.$$

Here are some examples to further demonstrate the application of simple interest.

If your firm borrows $200,000 to purchase new equipment for the warehouse, it will pay this amount back to the lending source in equal payments every month for 15 years, and the borrowed money is subject to a simple interest rate of 9.0 percent, what is the total of payments that will be made and how much does your firm need to pay every month?

The principle of $200,000 is subject to the interest rate of 9.0 percent. This implies that your firm, in addition to repaying $200,000, must also repay 9.0 percent of $200,000. To find 9.0 percent of $200,000, we multiply the decimal form of the interest rate (0.09) by the principle: $200,000 * 0.09 = $18,000. So the total owed is $200,000 + $18,000 = $218,000. To determine the amount that needs to be paid each month, we divide $218,000 by the total number of months that it will be paid in, $218,000 / (15 years * 12 months per year) = $218,000 / 180 = $1,211.11 every month.

If your firm, then, borrows $125,000 from the same bank to invest in company cars for the sales staff at a simple interest rate of 15 percent to be paid off every month for 5 years, how much must be repaid and what monthly amount does this represent?

The interest that will be repaid is found by multiplying the principle ($125,000) by the interest rate (15 percent or 0.15 in decimal form), $125,000 * 0.15 = $18,750. So the total to be repaid is $143,750, or $143,750 / 60 = $2,395.83 every month for 60 months (five years).

Compound interest

You have surely heard and read personal investment advice saying that getting out of debt quickly is extremely beneficial to your financial future. This is because most lending institutions do not lend money based upon simple interest. If they did, there would be no financial gain to repaying debt early, except to simply be out of debt. In fact, there may be some financial benefits to extending the payment terms, because inflation will decrease the value of money.

Money is usually lent upon the terms that interest will be compounded more than once—daily, weekly, monthly, biannually, or annually. Most banks and others who lend money do so based upon compound interest rates, usually with an interest rate that applies to a year. Similar to an interest on your credit card, where you are charged between 14 percent and 22 percent interest annually, a bank charges an interest rate for the year on money borrowed. When a loan is granted with compound interest, it means that during the course of the loan, interest is compounded many times during its repayment. A nominal rate of interest is calculated, depending on how often the loan is compounded. A nominal interest rate is an incremental interest rate.

For example, credit cards charge an interest rate per year, usually between 14 percent and 22 percent. This is not the rate that is applied to each billing cycle, though. The rate that is applied to each billing cycle is the annual rate divided by 12 if the billing cycle is a month.

If a $5,000 loan that will be paid monthly for a year at 10 percent interest is compounded biannually, the amount of money borrowed is subject to interest twice and the nominal interest rate is 5 percent. Initially, the entire amount will be subject to interest, then at six months, the amount that has yet to be paid plus the interest already accrued will be subject to interest. If the loan was borrowed on the first of January and interest is accrued on January 1st and July 1st, then the entire loan will be subject to 5 percent interest immediately and the balance of the account increases: Principle + (principle * 0.05) = $5,000 + ($5,000 * 0.05) = $5,000 + $250 = $5,250 (*or* principle * (1 + 0.05) = $5,000 * 1.05 = $5,250), so the value of the loan (to be repaid) is $5,250.

If payments totaling $3,000 are made by June 30th, before interest is accrued for the second time, then a total of $2,250 is subject to interest, and the amount to be repaid is $2,250 + ($2,250 * 0.05) = $2,250 + $112.50 = $2,362.50. If this were broken down into equal monthly payments to complete the payoff before further interest accrued, the six monthly payments would be $2,362.50 / 6 = $393.75 a month for the remaining six months.

From the above example, we have derived the fact that nominal interest applied to a loan is found by multiplying the nominal interest rate by the balance of the loan.

Here is another scenario involving compound interest that will further clarify how this type of interest is calculated.

If your firm borrows $10,000 at an interest rate of 10 percent compounded monthly for the three years it will take to pay it off, find the nominal rate and the balance of the loan at the beginning of the third months if payments of $500 are made each month.

The nominal interest rate is 10 percent / 12 = 0.83 percent, so the initial balance is $10,000 * (1 + 0.0083) = $10,000 * 1.0083 = $10,083. The first payment of $500 is made during the first month so the balance reduces to $10,083 − $500 = $9,583. Again, $9,583 is subject to the nominal interest rate of 0.83 percent so, the balance increases to $9,583 * 1.0083 = $9,662.54. During the second month, a payment of $500 reduces the balance of the account to $9,662.54 - $500 = $9,162.54. At the beginning of the third month, the balance is subject to the nominal interest rate and the balance increases to $9,162.54 * 1.0083 = $9,238.59.

Answer the questions in Sections A and B on the following pages to reinforce your understanding of simple and compound interest. The answers follow.

Section A

1. Find the monthly amount needed to repay a loan of $10,000 if it is subject to a simple interest rate of 7 percent and will be repaid monthly in equal amounts over a period of one year.

2. What is the total to be repaid to the bank on a loan of $65,800 paid monthly for five years at the interest rate of 12.2 percent?

3. Your firm borrows $458,000 and plans to repay monthly in equal amounts over 15 years at the interest rate of 9.2 percent. Unfortunately, your firm is not able to make the first two months payment and makes a deal with the bank that your firm will pay the amount over the rest of the loan frame by increasing its monthly payment. If there is no penalty for not making a payment, find the monthly total that is owed every month for the remainder of the loan's term.

4. Find the amount that was borrowed on a loan that is paid back over 12 months with monthly payments of $229.17 and you know that the interest rate is 10 percent.

5. Another possible application of simple interest is that the simple interest rate can be multiplied by the number of years. If you borrow $5,000 for a personal loan at a rate of 10 percent per year, and simple interest is calculated up front, what is the total that will be paid if the terms are over two years, and how much will each payment be if they are made monthly?

Section B

1. A firm borrows $4,000 from a bank at an interest rate of 10 percent compounded monthly. Find the balance on the account at the end of the second month if the firm pays $250 in each of the first two months.

2. The same firm borrows $200,000 from a different bank to overhaul its lagging sales force. The terms of the loan are as follows: The firm will repay the loan monthly with interest compounded annually at an annual interest rate of 12 percent and the firm will make monthly payments of $3,000 until the loan is paid. Find the nominal rate and the balance of the loan at the end of the second year.

3. Find the nominal interest rate for a loan compounded daily at an annual interest rate of 13 percent.

4. A firm borrows $10,000 from a bank at an annual interest rate of 10 percent compounded daily with a provision that states that the firm does not need to make any payments the first month. If the firm makes no payments during the first month, find the balance of the loan after the first 30 days.

Answers

Section A

1. $891.67
2. $73,827.60
3. $2,809.75. Hint: there are only 178 payment periods instead of the original 180.
4. $2,500. Hint: division is the inverse of multiplication so if you find the total that is paid back and divide that by 100 percent plus the interest rate, you can find the original amount.
5. $6,000 total, or $250 a month for 24 months.

Section B

1. $3,564.60
2. 12%, $174,560
3. ~0.036%
4. $(10,000) * (1.000273972)^{30} = (10,000) * 1.008252 = 10,082.52$

    Notice how the answer to this problem was calculated via the formula (Principle) * (1 + Nominal Interest Rate)$^{\text{Term periods without payment}}$.

Investment

Similar to term payments on a loan, investments in a bank (in the form of a savings account) can be compounded daily, weekly, monthly, biannually, or annually. If your firm has extra earnings that it will not use in the next few accounting cycles, it may be wise to invest it. A savings account is the simplest and most risk-averse investment and is generally compounded more than once a year.

If your firm invests $1,000,000 in a savings account that yields an interest of 4 percent annually and is compounded monthly, you can find the value of the account after that year using the following formula:

New account value = (principle value) * (Nominal interest rate)$^{\text{times interest compounded}}$ or New account value = PI^n.

The value of the money that your firm invested, provided none was added to the account or removed, is:

$1,000,000 * (1.003333)^{12} =$
$1,000,000 * (1.040737) = 1,040,737.39$

Complete the exercises in Section C to test your knowledge of how to calculate interest on an investment. The answers follow.

Section C

1. In a savings account that compounds interest monthly and pays an annual interest rate of three percent, I invest $3,000. Find the value of that account if I keep the money in it for two years and do not remove or add any money.

2. I invest in a risky savings program that pays 10 percent annually and compounds monthly if the company does not bankrupt. If I invest $10,000 and the company is still firm after three years, what is the value of my account?

3. Regarding problem number two, what is the value of my account after five years?

4. You invest $12,000 of your firm's money in a program that yields 7 percent annually compounded daily. After a year and a half, what is the value of the account.

Answers

1. ($3,000) * $(1.0025)^{24}$ = $3,185.27

2. ($10,000) * $(1.0083)^{36}$ = $13,465.78

3. ($10,000) * $(1.0083)^{60}$ = $16,420.49

4. ($12,000) * $(1.00019178)^{548}$ (547.5 is rounded up as the number of compounding periods) = $13, 329.67

Common Financial Ratios

In Chapter 8, you learned of a few financial ratios that can help you analyze a firm's financial position. The following are other commonly used ratios not included in Chapter 8.

Liquidity ratios

Liquidity ratios indicate the ease at which a firm can convert its assets into cash.

Quick or acid-test ratio: The ratio of current assets, minus inventory, to current liabilities. This ratio is useful in assessing a firm's liquidity with the least liquid asset—inventory—removed.

$$\text{Acid-Test Ratio} = \frac{\text{Current Assets} - \text{Inventory}}{\text{Current Liabilities}}$$

Individual current asset ratio: The ratio of each individual current asset to total current liabilities; determines the amount of liabilities that are financed by individual assets.

$$\text{Individual Current Asset Ratio} = \frac{\text{Each Current Asset}}{\text{Current Liabilities}}$$

Asset utilization: Activity and turnover ratios

Activity and turnover ratios show how effectively a firm manages its assets and how specific assets are helping the company and how liabilities are affecting it.

Accounts receivable turnover ratio: The ratio of annual credit sales to average accounts receivable; explains how efficiently a firm is managing its accounts receivable.

$$\text{Accounts Receivable Turnover Ratio} = \frac{\text{Annual Credit Sales}}{\text{Average Accounts Receivable}}$$

Average collection period ratio: The ratio of average accounts receivable to annual credit sales divided by 365. Dividing annual credit sales by 365 provides credit sales per day. Then by dividing accounts receivable by credit sales per day you arrive at the average length it takes to collect accounts receivable.

$$\text{Average Collection Period Ratio} = \frac{\text{Accounts Receivable}}{\text{Annual Credit Sales} / 365}$$

Profitability ratios

Profitability ratios reveal how profitable a firm is compared to sales, assets, etc.

Gross profit margin ratio: The ratio of sales minus cost of goods sold (i.e., materials, labor, manufacturing, overhead) to total sales. This ratio indicates how sales are being managed and the cost of goods sold relative to sales.

$$\text{Gross Profit Margin Ratio} = \frac{\text{Sales} - \text{Cost of Goods Sold}}{\text{Total Sales}}$$

Return on total assets ratio: The ratio of net profit to total assets. This ratio measures the profit the firm earns given its assets and indicates whether it is effectively utilizing its assets to generate profit.

$$\text{Return on Total Assets Ratio} = \frac{\text{Net Profit}}{\text{Total Assets}}$$

Total asset turnover ratio: The ratio of sales to total assets. This ratio indicates the amount of sales that are generated from the firm's assets and shows how useful assets are in relation to sales.

$$\text{Total Asset Turnover Ratio} = \frac{\text{Sales}}{\text{Total Assets}}$$

Fixed asset turnover ratio: The ratio of sales to fixed assets. (The term "fixed assets" refers to the firm's property, plant, and equipment shown on the balance sheet.) This ratio provides information about how successful the firm is in generating sales from specific assets.

$$\text{Fixed Asset Turnover Ratio} = \frac{\text{Sales}}{\text{Fixed Assets}}$$

Return on stockholders' equity ratio: The ratio of net profit to stockholders' equity. (This ratio is also known as the *net worth ratio.*) It indicates what kind of profit is being generated given an amount of owners' equity.

$$\text{Return on Stockholders' Equity Ratio} = \frac{\text{Net Profit}}{\text{Stockholders' Equity}}$$

Leverage ratios

The term "leverage" refers to how much debt a firm has. Leverage ratios compare this debt to other items on the income statement or the balance sheet.

Total debt to stockholders' equity ratio: The ratio of total debt to equity. This ratio shows owners of the firm how much total debt there is compared to the amounts they have invested.

$$\text{Total debt to Stockholders' Equity Ratio} = \frac{\text{Total Debt}}{\text{Stockholders' Equity}}$$

Times interest earned ratio: The ratio of earnings before interest and taxes to interest charges. This ratio determines if interest charges are covered by earnings before interest and taxes.

$$\text{Times Interest Earned Ratio} = \frac{\text{Earnings Before Interest \& Taxes}}{\text{Interest Charges}}$$

Section A

Based upon information in Tables VIII-1 and VIII-2 on pages 127 and 128, find the following financial ratios.

1. Acid-test ratio.
2. Individual current asset ratio for cash.
3. Individual current asset ratio for accounts receivable.
4. Individual current asset ratio for inventory.
5. Accounts receivable turnover ratio.
6. Average collection period ratio.
7. Gross profit margin ratio.
8. Return on total assets.
9. Total asset turnover ratio.
10. Fixed asset turnover.
11. Return on stockholders' equity ratio.
12. Total debt to stockholders' equity ratio.
13. Times interest earned ratio.

Answers

1.	100%	8.	3.67%
2.	44.4%	9.	1.43 times
3.	55.5%	10.	4.55 times
4.	166.6%	11.	5.83%
5.	10 times	12.	59.1%
6.	36.5 days	13.	9.76 times
7.	26.2%		

The Metric System

Let's face it, the United States is far behind measurement norms. The metric system is the international measurement system and, unlike the British system we have adopted, the metric system is easy to learn and use because it is based upon powers of 10. Like the base-10 system, the metric system organizes values into units of tens, and once a group is valued at 10, it becomes a part of a higher group. The metric system has prefixes that are attached to general measures of weight, length, and volume. You are probably familiar with the prefixes milli, centi, deci, deka, hecto, and kilo. They all represent a certain portion or total of the general measure, respectively, thousandth, hundredth, tenth, ten, hundred, and thousand. The term kilometer, used to measure length, for example, is 1,000 times the general measure, the meter, or 1,000 meters. The general measure of weight is the gram. Often you hear weight in terms of kilograms (1,000 grams) or milligrams (0.001 grams). The general measure of length is the meter and the general measure of volume is the liter. From each base measurement, we can formulate the following tables for weight, volume, and length:

Weight
Base: Gram

Prefix	Measurement	Part of base
milli	1 mg	0.001 gram
centi	1 cg	0.01 gram
deci	1 dg	0.1 gram
—	1 g	1 gram
deka	1 dag	10 grams
hecto	1 hg	100 grams
kilo	1kg	1,000 grams

Volume
Base: Liter

Prefix	Measurement	Part of Base
milli	1 m*l*	0.001 liter
centi	1 c*l*	0.01 liter
deci	1 d*l*	0.1 liter
—	1 *l*	1 liter
deka	1 da*l*	10 liters
hecto	1 h*l*	100 liters
kilo	1k*l*	1,000 liters

Length
Base: Meter

Prefix	Measurement	Part of Base
milli	1 mm	0.001 meter
centi	1 cm	0.01 meter
deci	1 dm	0.1 meter
—	1 m	1 meter
deka	1 dam	10 meters
hecto	1 hm	100 meters
kilo	1km	1,000 meters

Converting among measures of the metric system is quite simple. Multiplying or dividing by a power of 10 are the only two operations needed to transfer within a unit of measure. For example, if you buy two liters of soda at lunch and want to know how many centiliters you have, you need to multiply the number of liters (2, for example) by 100 because there are 100 centiliters in a liter (or there are 0.01 liters in a centiliter). A common, simple, and beneficial way to express this problem is with conversion factors like so:

$$2\ell \ = \ 2\ell \ * \frac{(100\ c\ell)}{(1\ell)} \quad = \quad 200c\ell$$

Similarly, you could create a conversion factor if you want to find your heights in terms of dekameters. Let's' say that you are 234 centimeters tall. Because there are 1,000 centimeters in a dekameter, the conversion factor looks like this:

$$234\ cm = 234\ cm * \frac{(1\ dam)}{(1,000\ cm)} = 0.234\ dam$$

Or you are 0.234 dekameters tall.

Conversion factors can also be used to change a measurement from the metric system to the British system or British to metric. The following charts will help you with conversions.

Weight

British	Metric
1 ounce	28.35 g
1 pound	0.45 kg
1 ton (2,000 lbs)	0.91 metric tons
2,222.22 lbs	1 metric ton
0.04 oz	1 g
2.22 lbs	1 kg

Volume

British	Metric
1 fluid ounce	29.57 m*l*
1 pint	0.47 *l*
1 quart	0.95 *l*
1 gallon	3.79 *l*
0.03 fl oz	1 m*l*
1.05 qt or 2.13 pt	1 *l*

Length

British	Metric
1 inch	2.54 cm
1 foot	30.48 cm or 3.05 dm
1 yard	0.91 m
1 mile	1.61 km or 1609 m
0.39 in	1 cm
39.37 in or 3.28 ft or1.09 yd	1 m
0.62 mi	1 km

Index